Introduction

Exam Guidance

Post-1914 Prose: Short Stories

Pre-1914 and Post-1914 Poetry

This edition of *AQA GCSE English Literature* is matched to the AQA GCSE English Literature Specification A, covering the short stories, pre-1914 poetry, and post-1914 poems by Duffy and Armitage from the AQA Anthology.

As a revision guide, it focuses on the material which is externally assessed and includes all the information students need to pass the exam.

Students following this course will sit one exam paper which is divided into two sections – Section A: post-1914 prose (short stories from the Anthology), and Section B: pre-1914 and post-1914 poetry from the Anthology. This guide is divided up in the same way to allow students to prepare for each section separately.

Each section of the guide begins with an overview of that part of the exam: what will be tested, the time allowed to answer the question, and the number and format of the questions.

An overview of the exam as a whole is given at the beginning of the book.

'Exam Practice' and 'Exam Preparation' tasks are included throughout to help students prepare for the exam and practise their skills, along with hints and tips to help them succeed.

Additional useful information is given, including how to structure writing, correct usage of punctuation, grammar and spelling, and a list of language terms, which will help students to produce good, coherent answers. This appears at the beginning of the book, along with further information relevant to both sections of the exam. It is hoped that this will provide a useful reference when studying for either section of the exam.

AQA GCSE English Literature is written by Paul Burns and Jan Edge, who are both teachers and examiners. Between them, they have 30 years' experience of teaching English at Key Stage 4. In addition, their experience as GCSE examiners means that they have an excellent understanding of the criteria used for marking English Literature papers and are able to offer invaluable advice on how to perform well in the exam.

Another edition of this revision guide is available which covers the short stories, pre-1914 poetry, and post-1914 poems by Heaney and Clarke. For more information, contact Customer Services quoting 1-905896-03-5.

Contents

Exam Overview

The AQA GCSE English Literature exam consists of one paper which will last for 1 hour and 45 minutes. The paper is divided into two sections: prose (Section A) and poetry (Section B).

In preparation for Section A, you will study either a post-1914 novel from the list of set texts (chosen for you by your teachers), or the short stories in the AQA Anthology. This revision guide covers only the short stories from the Anthology. For Section B, you will study pre-1914 poetry by a selection of poets, and post-1914 poetry by Seamus Heaney and Gillian Clarke or Carol Ann Duffy and Simon Armitage. This revision guide covers only the poems by Duffy and Armitage.

The exam is worth 70% of your total mark for English Literature (see table below).

Up to three marks are available for the quality of written communication, i.e. how successfully you can communicate your ideas in writing. To obtain maximum marks for written communication, make sure that...
- the information you give is relevant
- the information you give is presented coherently – paragraphs and information should be in a logical order
- your writing is legible
- your punctuation, grammar and spelling are accurate.

(See pages 5–7 for advice on how to produce high-quality written answers.)

The Questions

Read the exam paper and each question very carefully. Make sure you understand exactly what the question is asking you to do before you begin to answer it.

You must make it very clear which question you are answering in the exam. Clearly write the number of the question you have chosen to answer.

The Anthology

You will have been given an Anthology at the beginning of your AQA GCSE English Literature course. You will probably have used this Anthology to highlight and make notes on the short stories and poems.

Remember that you will not be able to take your annotated Anthology into the exam. You will be given a clean copy of the Anthology in the exam.

Helpful Hints

Remember that the information in this revision guide is not intended to replace what you have learned in class, just to provide you with key points to help with your revision.

Try to stay calm in the exam and enjoy writing your answers.

Section	Section Title	Questions	Time Allowed	Percentage of Mark
A	Post-1914 Prose (Short Stories)	Answer one question	45 minutes	30%
B	Pre-1914 Poetry, and Post-1914 Poetry by Duffy and Armitage	Answer one question	1 hour	40%

Structure and Paragraphs

In the English Literature exam, the examiners will want to see well-structured answers. This means presenting your answers neatly and writing your answers in a structure and style that clearly make the points you are trying to convey.

Structure

Structure refers to the way your answers are organised, and the way that your ideas are developed through the paragraphs. When you write an answer, it is important that you structure it well. This is why it is beneficial to spend some time planning your answers before you begin (see page 10).

Paragraphs

The examiner will be looking for evidence of paragraphs when marking your paper. Paragraphs are used to organise pieces of writing: they are sets of sentences which contain related ideas or subjects.

Using paragraphs means you do not end up with a solid block of text, and it allows you to present your answers in an organised way so that your points are easier to follow.

You should begin a new paragraph every time you start to write about something new.

You can create paragraphs by leaving a line before starting a new paragraph, or by indenting the text when you start a new paragraph. For example…

> The setting helps to show how relationships with others around us, and the world, change as we get older.
>
> The theme of change runs through both stories…

> The setting helps to show how relationships with others around us, and the world, change as we get older.
>
>   The theme of change runs through both stories…

Linking Paragraphs

Connectives are words and phrases which can be used to link paragraphs (or sentences within paragraphs). They help your writing to flow.

This list provides you with some connectives that you could use when writing your answers in the exam. Try to think of some more of your own.

- However…
- On the other hand…
- Although…
- Equally…
- Similarly…
- In addition…
- In contrast…
- In conclusion…

Punctuation, Grammar and Spelling

Correct use of punctuation and grammar is very important in order to convey clear meaning through a piece of writing. The following information is provided to help you when you are writing your answers in the English Literature exam (and in your other exams). Read the information through and make sure you understand it. You will be expected to use punctuation and grammar correctly in your written answers.

Full Stops (.)

Full stops separate sentences. Without them, writing does not make sense.

Commas (,)

A comma can be used to join two sentences into one, but it must be followed by a connecting word such as 'while', 'yet' or 'but', for example…
– He is bitter and spiteful, but he loves his family.

Commas are used to mark off parts of a sentence which give extra information, but are not necessary for the sentence to make sense, for example…
– Alice, his granddaughter, could be seen as selfish. The highlighted phrase and commas could be taken out and the sentence would still make sense.

Commas are also used to list items, for example…
– The old man is described as old-fashioned, bitter, stubborn and lonely.

Question Marks (?)

Question marks come at the end of questions, for example…
– Could the old woman be envious of the younger generation?   ✓
– He asked if the old woman could be envious of the younger generation?   ✗

Colons (:)

Colons are used before an example or explanation, for example…
– The poet uses onomatopoeia to describe the water: it 'trickles'.

Colons also appear before a list, for example…
– The poet has used many language techniques: alliteration, assonance and personification.

The part before the colon must be a complete sentence, but the part after it does not need to be.

Semi-colons (;)

Semi-colons are used to show that two sentences are closely related, for example…
– In *Growing Up*, childhood is portrayed through the adult's eyes; in *Snowdrops*, it is portrayed through the child's eyes.

The parts before and after the semi-colon must be complete sentences.

Apostrophes (')

Apostrophes are used to show omission or contraction (usually in speech or in informal writing). The apostrophe replaces the missing letter(s), for example…
– He didn't want anything to change.
  (didn't = did not)
– He's finished his work but she's still doing hers.
  (he's = he has, she's = she is)

Apostrophes are also used to show possession. If the owner is singular (or plural but does not end in 's', e.g. sheep, men, children), add an apostrophe and an 's' to the word that indicates the owner, for example…
– The boy's grandfather. (i.e. the grandfather of the boy.)
– The girl's shoes. (i.e. the shoes of the girl.)
– The children's games. (i.e. the games of the children.)

If there is more than one owner (plural) and the word indicating the owners ends in 's', simply add an apostrophe at the end, for example…
– The boys' grandfather. (i.e. the grandfather of the boys.)
– The girls' shoes. (i.e. the shoes of the girls.)

Confusing Words

The following words are often used incorrectly. Make sure you know the correct way to use each one.

Done / did, and seen / saw

– He did it	✓	– He saw it	✓
– He has done it	✓	– He has seen it	✓
– He done it	✗	– He seen it	✗

Could, would, should, ought to, might, may, can, will

These are modal verbs. They are never followed by 'of'; they are followed by 'have', for example…

– She should have looked after her family.	✓
– She should of looked after her family.	✗

It is important that you spell and use words correctly in your answers in the exam. The following list contains words which are frequently misused. It will help you if you read through these words and learn the correct ways to spell and use them.

Accept	– to receive: 'he accepts the man's apology'.
Except	– apart from: 'they were all playing, except the girl'.
Its	– belonging to it: 'the eagle spread its wings'.
It's	– short for 'it is' (the apostrophe shows that the 'i' is missing): 'it's a sad poem'.
No	– opposite of 'yes': 'no, I don't like it'.
Know / knew	– being aware of something: 'he didn't know the girl knew about it'.
New	– opposite of old: 'it's a new story'.
Passed	– a verb: 'I passed all my GCSEs'.
Past	– a noun indicating a previous time: 'the story is set in the past'. (Also used in phrases such as 'he went past' or 'they are past their best'.)
Practice	– a noun: 'exam practice can be very helpful'.
Practise	– a verb: 'if you practise writing answers, you should do well in the exam'. (The same rule applies to advice / advise and licence / license.)

There	– in that place: 'he is there'. (Also used in phrases such as 'there is', 'there are', etc.)
Their	– belonging to them: 'they left their family home'.
They're	– 'they are' (the apostrophe shows that the 'a' is missing): 'they're not happy anymore'.
Too	– excessively: 'the girl is too selfish'.
Two	– the number: 'he saw two flowers'.
To	– towards: 'he went to school'. ('To' is also part of the infinitive of a verb: 'to do', 'to think', etc.)
Where	– a place: 'where is it?'.
Wear	– used with clothes, etc.: 'she had to wear a coat'.
We're	– 'we are' (the apostrophe shows that the 'a' is missing): 'we're not sure'.
Were	– past tense of the verb 'to be': 'they were walking to the lake'.
Whether	– if: 'it is not clear whether it refers to the girl or to her mother'.
Weather	– the sun, wind, rain, etc.: 'the weather often reflects the characters' moods'.
Whose	– belonging to whom: 'whose book is it?'.
Who's	– 'who is' or 'who has' (the apostrophe shows that the 'i' or 'ha' is missing): 'who's that boy?', 'who's dropped that book?'.

Language Terms

The following is a list of language terms. You will have used these terms in class to describe the techniques that writers use in their work. This list is a reminder of the main techniques and why a writer might use them.

The terms are mentioned throughout the revision guide, so it will help you to read them before you start revising the short stories and poems. (See also page 15 and page 37.)

Adjectives: describe nouns, e.g. great, harsh, excruciating. *Used to add more detail to the noun, and to build images in the reader's mind.*

Adverbs: describe verbs (the action) and often end with -ly, e.g. carefully, quietly, quickly. *Used to add more detail to a description of an action.*

Alliteration: repetition of a sound at the beginning of words, e.g. 'river rushing rapidly'. *Used to stress certain words or phrases.*

Ambiguity: a sentence or word which has more than one possible meaning (it is ambiguous). *Used to express more than one meaning at once, and to make the reader think.*

Assonance: rhyme of the internal vowel sound, e.g. 'fresh' and 'wet', 'sad' and 'black'. *Used to slow the reader down and emphasise certain words.*

Colloquial language: informal language, e.g. language used in everyday conversation. It may use local dialect words / phrases. *Used to indicate relationships between characters and to create an informal tone.*

Connotation: the meaning that is suggested by the use of a particular word, e.g. red could indicate danger. *Used to make a point in a subtle way.*

Contrast: a strong difference between two things. *Used to highlight differences.*

Exclamations: show anger, shock, horror, surprise and joy, e.g. 'I won!'. *Used to portray emotions.*

Imagery: words that are so descriptive they allow you to create a picture in your mind. *Used to involve the reader in the moment being described.*

Irony and sarcasm: the use of words to imply the opposite of their meaning. *Used to make fun of people or issues.*

Juxtaposition: the positioning of two contrasting words, phrases or ideas next to or near each other. *Used to highlight a contrast.*

Metaphor: an image created by referring to something as something else, e.g. 'the army of ants'. Here the ants are referred to as an army. *Used to give additional information to the reader to create a particular effect or to emphasise a point.*

Onomatopoeia: a word that sounds like what it describes, e.g. splash, boom, click. *Used to appeal to the reader's sense of hearing.*

Oxymoron: two contradictory terms placed together, e.g. 'bitter sweet', 'cruel kindness'. *Used to make each term stand out and to highlight a contrast.*

Personification: making an object or animal sound like a person, giving it human qualities, e.g. 'the fingers of the tree grabbed at her hair'. *Used to help the reader to identify with what is being personified and helps to create a specific image.*

Questions (interrogatives): show that the writer wants the reader to consider a question, or that they themselves are considering a question. *Used to show a range of things about a character, such as inquisitiveness, upset and confusion.*

Pathetic fallacy: when the surroundings (e.g. the weather) reflect the mood of the character. *Used to create mood and atmosphere in the writing.*

Repetition: when words, phrases, sentences or structures are repeated. *Used to stress certain words or key points in the writing.*

Rhetorical questions: questions that do not need an answer, e.g. when your teachers ask, 'do you think that is funny?' they do not expect you to answer. *Used to make the reader think about the question that has been asked.*

Rhythm: the beat of the writing (especially poetry): fast or slow, regular or irregular. *Used to create atmosphere, and to add to the overall effect.*

Simile: a comparison of one thing to another that includes the word 'as' or 'like', e.g. 'the man was as cold as ice', 'the pain was like a searing heat'. *Used to give additional information to the reader to create a particular effect or to emphasise a point.*

Standard English: the conventional use of words and grammar in the English language.

Superlatives: words which express the best or worst of something. They often end in *-est* or have 'most' or 'least' before them, e.g. 'lowest', 'happiest', 'most beautiful', 'least stylish'. *Used to emphasise a point.*

Symbols and symbolism: a symbol is an object which represents something else – often an abstract idea, e.g. a dove symbolises peace. *Used to create a stronger, more vivid image, or to communicate an idea indirectly.*

Tone: the overall attitude of the writing, e.g. formal, informal, sad, playful, angry, suspicious, ironic. *Used to allow the emotions of the author, or the characters in the writing, to be expressed.*

Helpful Hint

It is good to be able to use these terms with confidence, but remember that you should always explain the effect that these techniques have on the reader (you).

Planning and Checking

For example, a plan based on the following question could look like this:

Q. Compare how childhood is portrayed in *Growing Up* and *Snowdrops*.

Compare…
- the different experiences of childhood
- how childhood is portrayed through the way the writers write and the language they use.

Plan

Intro: childhood in 'Snowdrops' and 'Growing Up' portrayed differently. In 'Growing' Up', childhood portrayed through adult's eyes; in 'Snowdrops', portrayed through child's eyes.

Structure: both end with characters being disappointed.

Style: war imagery in 'Growing Up', contrasts with childish imagery (similes) in 'Snowdrops'.

Direct, abrupt speech in 'Growing Up' contrasts with childlike, enthusiastic speech in 'Snowdrops'.

Settings: similar – home / garden – familiar, family places. 'Growing Up' – wild garden reflects girls' personalities. 'Snowdrops' – cold day reflects death.

Themes: theme of change in both – children are growing up.

Conclusion: each portrays childhood differently but effectively. Warm to characters in 'Snowdrops' more.

In each section of the exam, you should spend about five minutes planning your answer, and a few minutes at the end checking your answer.

The Importance of Planning

It is very important and very beneficial to plan your answers. Examiners like to see that you have planned your work. A plan reminds you to structure your work in paragraphs, and helps you to produce a good answer which is clear, logical and flows well.

When you have chosen your question, read it through a few times so that you understand exactly what you are being asked to do. Pay particular attention to the bullet points. Underline the key words and the titles of the texts that you are being asked to write about. With the question in mind, read the texts that you will be writing about. Highlight any parts that you may want to refer to or quote. Note down any thoughts you have, then try to put them in order of how you will discuss them in your answer.

The Importance of Checking

Checking your work is equally as important as planning. Allow yourself a few minutes at the end of the exam for checking. Read your answers carefully and ensure you have covered everything you wanted to. Check that the words you have used put across the exact idea or point that you intended them to.

Check your spelling and punctuation – it is easy to make mistakes when you are under pressure. (Ensure that you learn and understand the punctuation, grammar and spelling tips on pages 6–7.)

Helpful Hints

Make sure you label your plan as such, so that the examiners know it is not part of your final answer.

If, when you are checking your work, you find a mistake, put a neat line through it and write the correct version above or alongside.

When responding to the short stories and poems in the exam, you must show the examiner that you can do the following:

- **Respond to texts critically, sensitively and in detail, using textual evidence as appropriate.**
  This means that you must explore the characters' feelings, their relationships and their situations, and analyse how they are presented through the language used. You must use the PEE technique (point, evidence, explanation): make a point about the text with reference to the question, use a quote to back up the point that you make, or refer to a section of the text, and then explain what the quote or reference says about the text.

- **Explore how language, structure and form contribute to the meanings of the texts and consider different interpretations of the texts.**
  This means that you have to look at the words, phrases and sentences that the writer uses: the way that the text is set out – the beginning, middle and end; and the form, i.e. the type or genre of writing that the writer uses, for example, a sonnet, free verse, etc. (see page 12).

  You have to be able to interpret each text on many levels. Identify all the things that it could mean – the obvious meanings and what the writer implies through tone and language. Give a personal response – suggest your own ideas and interpretations.

- **Explore relationships and comparisons between texts, selecting and evaluating relevant material.**
  This means that you must understand what the short stories or poems have in common and in which ways they differ. You must be able to find relationships between them and compare and contrast them (see page 13).

- **Relate texts to their social, cultural and historical contexts and literary traditions.**
  This means that you must be able to write about the social relationships that the characters in the short stories and poems have with each other and with the societies in which they live; the cultures that are depicted; the period of time in which the texts were written or set; and the traditions and ways of life that were normal to people in that place and at that time. You should also be able to comment on any literary traditions (see page 12). You should be able to suggest how all these things influence the text.

The PEE Technique

When you respond to the short stories and poems in the exam, you are required to use the PEE technique (**P**oint, **E**vidence, **E**xplanation). For example…

P In *Growing Up*, it is evident in the opening paragraphs that the father adores his children.

E We are told that he 'missed his two small girls and looked forward eagerly to their greeting'.

E He is a good, loving father. The adverb 'eagerly' stresses that he cannot wait to see them.

Helpful Hint

Try to include your own personal response in your answers. For example, you could say whether you think something is portrayed in a clearer way in one short story or poem than in the other(s), etc.

Style, Structure and Form

Style, structure and form are linked when you are studying a short story or poem. They all contribute to the overall meaning and effect.

Style

Style refers to the language used in the short story or poem. It is the overall effect created by the words that the writer has used and the way in which they have been used. This includes the tone that is created, the use of imagery and description, and the use of language techniques, e.g. alliteration, personification, metaphors, similes.

You should be able to use the terms on pages 8–9, 15 and 37 to describe the language and style of a short story or poem. (The terms on page 15 are more specific to describing prose; the terms on page 37 are more specific to describing poetry.) You should use these terms in your answers, whilst using the PEE technique and referring to the question that has been asked.

Structure

Structure refers to the order and arrangement of the short story or poem, e.g. is the opening gloomy, the middle part hopeful and the ending happy? Is the story or poem split into sub-sections or verses? Does it have a title or sub-headings? How is punctuation used? Look at the layout of the words on the page, font sizes, the length of sentences / lines and the length and order of paragraphs / verses, etc.

In poetry, structure also refers to the shape of the verses, and the rhythm and rhyme patterns in the poems.

The structure can have an impact on the overall meaning.

Form

Form refers to how the story or poem is written. For example, the basic form of the prose in the Anthology is the short story, but short stories can take many forms, e.g. a fairy story, a fable, a diary entry, etc. In poetry, there are many different forms, such as the sonnet, the monologue, free verse, etc.

Literary traditions are part of the form. They are traditional or typical features of particular forms, e.g. a fable has a moral to the story, action adventure stories usually have a hero, sonnets are usually addressed to a loved one.

Helpful Hint

When you are writing about the style of the short stories and poems, do not simply list all the techniques used. Make sure that you show your understanding of how the writer uses these techniques to create effects.

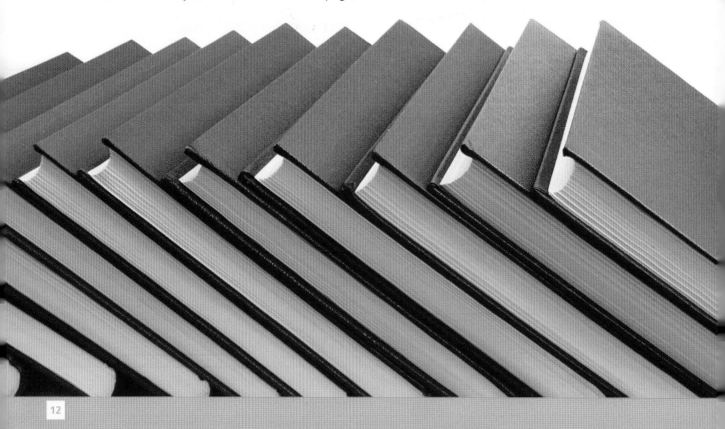

Relationships and Comparisons

You must be able to write about the relationships between the short stories, and the relationships between the poems. This means showing that you are aware of how they are similar, and how they are different. Their similarities may be in their themes, their settings, their attitudes, the messages they are communicating, the way they are written, the techniques used to create effects, etc.

In order to be able to compare the texts successfully, you need to fully understand each short story and poem and be aware of the main ideas in each. This means spending plenty of time reading and studying the short stories and poems and thinking carefully about the style, structure, form, themes, messages, feelings, attitudes, etc. of each one.

Every question in Section A of the exam will ask you to compare prose, and every question in Section B of the exam will ask you to compare poems, so it is important that you are able to do it well. You will be asked to compare two, three or more short stories or poems. The more short stories and poems that you are very familiar with, the greater choice of questions you will have in the exam that you can answer successfully.

When comparing texts, you must refer back to them in order to help you plan your answer, to find points to refer to, and to choose words and phrases to quote in your answer.

The example questions opposite will give you an idea of what you may be asked to do.

Example Question: Section A

Q. Compare how child–adult relationships are portrayed in *Your Shoes* and *Chemistry*.

Compare…
* the relationships between children and adults.
* how the relationships are portrayed through the way the writers write and the language they use.

Example Question: Section B

Q. Compare how attitudes to youth are shown in four of the poems you have read. Choose two poems from **List A** and two poems from **List B**.

List A
Before You Were Mine (Duffy)
We Remember Your Childhood Well (Duffy)
My father thought (Armitage)

List B
The Affliction of Margaret (Wordsworth)
The Little Boy Lost and *The Little Boy Found* (Blake)
Ulysses (Tennyson)

Remember to compare…
* how attitudes to youth are shown in the poems
* how these attitudes are conveyed through the poets' use of language.

Helpful Hint

Make sure that every point you make in your answer is relevant to the question.

Overview of Section A

Section A of the Exam: Post-1914 Prose

The prose section of your English Literature exam will test your knowledge of post-1914 prose.

This revision guide covers only the short stories from the Anthology for Section A of the exam. So, all the information given in this part of the revision guide will be based on answering a question on the short stories.

You will have 45 minutes to write your answer; you should spend approximately 5 minutes planning what you will write.

You will have to answer one question. You will have three questions to choose from. Read each question carefully and make sure you choose a question that you fully understand and that you are confident you can answer well.

The Questions

The question you choose to answer will follow one of these formats:
- The question will name two short stories and you will be asked to compare aspects of these texts.
- The question will name one short story and you will be asked to compare aspects of this text to another short story of your choice from the Anthology.

Helpful Hints

If the question only names one short story and you are asked to compare it to a text of your choice, be careful to choose a text that you know well and can write a lot about that is relevant to the question.

Read the bullet points in the question carefully; they are there to help you.

The following pages (pages 16–29) look at each short story in detail. You will have studied them thoroughly in class. This section will help you to revise the texts so that you are ready to answer your chosen question in the exam.

Reading and Analysing Prose

You will have read the short stories in class and annotated them with the help of your teacher. Do not fall into the trap of thinking that, therefore, you have studied them sufficiently. To do well, you must really know the stories so spend some time on your own reading them carefully.

The first time you read a short story you will get a sense of what is happening in the story. This is the **narrative**. You must read the story again closely to be able to comment upon **themes**, **characters**, **setting**, **structure and form**, **language and style**. You will have studied important aspects relating to these things in class or as part of independent study.

Themes

The theme is the subject of the text, e.g. friendship, the innocence of childhood, relationships between people, how life changes, etc. We can often get an idea of how the author feels about certain situations from the theme(s) in the story.

Characters

The characters are the people in the story. You must determine what the characters are like – refer to what they say and do, how they react to others and how they respond to situations. The way that the author writes about them will tell you what they are like: the writer may like or dislike a character, or may just depict him / her objectively (i.e. without giving an opinion).

Settings

The setting refers to where and when the story takes place. This can be the place (e.g. a house, a field, a country), the time period (e.g. the future, the 1800s, the present), the time in a character's life (e.g. childhood, old age), or the cultural setting (e.g. in a Muslim or Jewish household, around a Victorian dining table).

Structure and Style

Structure and style refer to how the text is organised and how it is written, and the way in which the author uses language (see language terms, pages 8–9).

The following list gives some style and structure terms that you may need to use when answering a question on the short stories.

Prose Terms

Authorial voice (authorial intrusion): the author makes an appeal to the reader by addressing him / her directly, e.g. using the pronoun 'you'. It is used to get the reader involved in the text, usually directly involved in the life of a character being described.

Diction: word choice. Are the words colloquial, simple, technical, ornate, modern or old-fashioned? Look at the word classes used, e.g. adjectives, adverbs, present participle verbs, etc.

Emotive language: the use of words that appeal to our emotions, e.g. if a girl is described as 'sad and lonely', we could deduce that the writer feels sorry for her and is inviting the reader to do so too.

Mood: the overall feel of the text. This may be created by how a character is feeling – sad, confused, hopeful, etc.

Narrative point of view: the author's opinion on a subject, conveyed through the choice of words applied to the subject. This can often be seen through the tone, e.g. criticism, enthusiasm, sentimentality, or with emotional detachment.

Register: the tone of the writing, e.g. formal, informal, conversational, biblical, written using archaic diction, etc.

Syntax: the arrangement of words – sentence structure and grammatical forms. Sentences could be simple and short, or complex and highly structured.

Tone: the mood of the text, for example, happy, concerned, satirical, ironic, involved, detached, etc.

You should also consider...
- the **purpose**: the reason the text was written, e.g. to inform, to instruct, to persuade, to entertain, to amuse or to portray a lifestyle. Also consider the writer's purpose: why the writer has written the text in a certain way, e.g. to tell the story of a person's misfortunes to evoke pity for him / her
- the **effect on the reader (you)**: how the reader reacts to certain aspects of the text. This can be manipulated by the writer's use of language.

Helpful Hint

When you are thinking about the setting of a story, think about the social, historical and cultural contexts.

Flight Doris Lessing

The Author

Doris Lessing was born to English parents in Persia (now Iran) in 1919. She grew up on a farm in Africa and had many jobs before becoming a professional writer. She married twice before the age of 30, but both marriages failed.

Narrative

Flight tells the story of an old man who lives with his daughter and her family, and keeps homing pigeons. He loves his birds and marvels at what they can do.

It is a close-knit family, and three generations live together. The youngest girl is set to marry the postmaster's son. All her sisters also married young – this tells us about social aspects of the family.

The man adores his granddaughter but he cannot come to terms with the fact that she is growing up and has a boyfriend, whom she is going to marry.

The story examines the old man's feelings and his relationships with his granddaughter and his daughter.

Setting

The action takes place in the garden and in the home of the characters – places associated with family and happiness. The dovecote is the place where the old man feels secure, loved and in control. The pigeons respect him and always return to him (even though it appears that members of his family do not and will not).

Narrative Structure

The story opens with a paragraph of positive diction describing the birds: 'rainbows', 'young', 'bright'. The beauty and tranquillity of the garden is stressed through positive words: 'rich', 'green', 'blossoms'.

This positive opening reflects the old man's mood at the beginning of the story: he is happy and content. However, when he notices his granddaughter looking towards the village, his mood changes. He becomes confrontational and aggressive, which contrasts with the opening of the story. He even becomes annoyed with his pigeons.

In the second half of the story there is a lot of direct speech as the old man's character, and his relationship with his daughter, are revealed. We also see that the young couple is aware of the distress they cause the old man so they bring him a new pigeon. They are trying to reassure him that nothing will change when they are married, but the writer's use of 'lying' shows that the old man knows this will not be the case.

At the end of the story, night time is falling. This symbolises the passage of time, change in life and the changes that relationships undergo.

Themes

- Family relationships.
- Different generations: how the older generation is regarded by the younger generations and vice versa
- Changing relationships.
- Love and jealousy.
- Unhappiness: the man is unhappy about his granddaughter's decision to marry.
- Being in control: the old man feels he has lost control of his family – they do what they want.
- Growing up: the old man's granddaughter is growing up.

Characters

The **old man** is loving and protective but has old-fashioned views. He regards his granddaughter as one of his birds and asks if he can keep her a bit longer. He is stubborn and can be spiteful. His exclamatory sentences indicate his anger. He was 'hating' himself, which suggests that he is bitter but doesn't want to be.

The **old man's granddaughter (Alice)** is in love and has become selfish because of it. She finds her grandad old-fashioned. She is rude towards him, ignoring his reprimands and the threats that he will tell her mother she is waiting for her boyfriend. However, she is also loving and considerate. This is shown when she gives her grandad a bird. At the end of the story she is upset as she knows that her life and her relationships are about to change forever and that she has lost her childhood.

The **old man's daughter (Lucy)** is blamed by the old man for encouraging the girls to marry young. He feels that she does not value him. She grows tired of the old man's protests. She humours the old man and speaks to him almost as if he were a child (lines 77 and 79). But she is kind and stresses to her father that he will still see his granddaughter every day. As their conversation progresses she loses patience with him and speaks to him 'coldly'.

The **postmaster's son (Steven)** is the granddaughter's boyfriend. He is not described in terms of his character. He symbolises any young man in this type of situation.

Structure and Style

- The title of the story has **multiple meanings** as it denotes the real flight of one of the old man's pigeons; the **metaphorical image** of flight representing freedom; the flight of his granddaughter from childhood to adulthood; and his flight from reality – refusing to face up to the truth that his granddaughter is growing up.
- **Short**, **direct sentences** are used to stress points and indicate the characters' moods.
- The opening paragraphs contain **positive diction** and are very descriptive. This sets the scene and reflects the old man's good mood at the beginning of the story.

- **Pathetic fallacy**: the weather conditions often reflect the characters' feelings and emotions.
- **Confrontational language**, with exclamatory sentences, shows the old man's anger and disappointment.
- **Direct speech** portrays the awkward relationship between the old man and his daughter.
- The story uses an **extended image** of the girl as a homing pigeon which will be set free to fly away – but she will not return as loyally as the homing pigeons.
- The use of **adverbs** highlights the characters' feelings, e.g. 'incredulously', 'coldly'.
- A **metaphor** runs throughout the story: the meaning of the word 'flight' in relation to the old man's granddaughter and his pigeons.

Superman... Sylvia Plath

The Author

Sylvia Plath was born in 1932 in Boston, America. She married English poet Ted Hughes but they later separated. She suffered from mental illness and committed suicide in 1963, aged just 30.

Narrative

Superman and Paula Brown's New Snowsuit is about a girl's memories of when she was young. She was obsessed with flying and dreamed about it every night. She dreamed that Superman visited her and taught her how to fly.

The girl recalls that she and her friend, David Sterling, made up stories on their way to school, and she remembers the games that they played at school. She was happy and contented in her childhood.

The girl recalls that she was invited to Paula Brown's birthday party, just before Christmas. Paula received a snowsuit that the girl describes in detail. Paula loved the snowsuit. One day, when they were all playing tag, Jimmy Lane caused Paula to fall in a patch of oil, spoiling her new snowsuit. Because Paula was fond of Jimmy and did not want to get him into trouble, she blamed the girl (the narrator of the story). The other children sided with Paula and accused the girl of pushing Paula over.

When David told the girl's mother that she was to blame, she was devastated by his betrayal and by the fact that her Uncle Frank would think badly of her. Frank said they would buy Paula another snowsuit to make everybody happy, but it did not make the girl happy. He also said that in ten years time no one would ever know the difference, but the girl still remembers the incident vividly and how it made her feel.

The story ends with the girl reflecting that this was the year that many things changed – the war began and she realised that life was not all dreams and happiness, that children could be cruel and that adults could be wrong. She was forced to grow up and leave behind her Superman dreams and sheltered childhood.

Setting

The story is set in Boston, America, when the girl is in the fifth grade at school. The events take place around home and school – places of childhood memories.

The story is set in the year that the Second World War broke out (1939). Throughout the story, the war and its consequences are alluded to – the air raids, the children pretending to be Nazis, and the war films at the cinema. The girl was so deeply affected by the scenes in the film that they made her physically sick.

Narrative Structure

The story begins with the girl recalling her happy childhood dreams, her friendships, her relationships with her mother and Uncle Frank, and the games she played at school. It is a happy time for her.

As the story progresses, the constant references to the war suggest that things are about to change and become less positive. After Paula's party, which is described in glowing terms (like Paula's snowsuit), things change and life for the girl becomes less happy and less simple.

When the girl is accused of spoiling the snowsuit, reality, betrayal and deceit intervene and the diction changes and becomes darker: 'cold', 'grey', 'blurred'. There is a great contrast between the current situation and the girl's life before – when she was happy in her dream world, playing childish games.

The story ends by repeating the line used to open the story but, at that time, the girl was happy. At the end, the same words are used but here they stress the negativity of the situation with the references to the 'real world' and the 'difference'.

Themes

- Family relationships – especially her relationship with Uncle Frank whom she admires and compares to her hero, Superman.
- Change – in relationships (the deceit of David and how she feels let down by Uncle Frank), and in the world around us.
- Childhood and growing up.
- The impact of war.
- Unhappiness – the girl is upset by her friend's disloyalty, being let down by Uncle Frank, and by the images of war.
- Friendship and loyalty.
- Things not being what they seem: the real world versus the imagination.

Characters

The main character is **the girl**, the narrator (or the persona). She is imaginative, playful and she forms childlike attachments to her peers. She is perceptive – she notices a change in the conversations between her mother and Uncle Frank as they discuss the war with foreboding (dread), and she realises that things are changing in her life. She is sensitive – she cries at

the suffering of the prisoners of war in the film and she dreams about them (instead of Superman). She is resolute – she will not admit to something that she has not done, even if it would save her from the disapproval she feels from Uncle Frank after she is accused of pushing Paula Brown.

Structure and Style

- The story could be **autobiographical** – it is written in the **first person** and the events are written through the narrator's perception. She is writing 13 years after the event happened but she describes how she perceived things as a child.
- **Short sentences** are used to represent the short space of time in which things can change.
- The story is very **descriptive** – the vivid dreams, the description of her school and the descriptions of Paula's snowsuit. The girl describes her own feelings and the other characters in immense detail.
- The **diction** and **images** move from positive ones ('technicolour') to more negative ones. The diction becomes darker as the images of war invade the text, e.g. in lines 180 and 181. It is as if the war invades the girl's life.
- **Imagery** is used to evoke strong memories (e.g. in line 4 and line 18).
- Heavy use of **adjectives** and **adverbs** to describe places such as the playground in line 31 and feelings, e.g. in line 155.
- **Pathetic fallacy**: descriptions of the weather reflect the girl's feelings.
- **Similes** paint vivid visual **images** of the feelings and scenes that she describes, e.g. she compares Paula's oil-soaked mittens to cat's fur.

Helpful Hint

A 'persona' is a character who is also the narrator in a story or poem. The persona in this story is the girl.

Exam Preparation

Make a collection of the descriptive phrases that are used throughout this story and use them to practise the PEE technique.

Your Shoes Michèle Roberts

The Author

Michèle Roberts was born in 1949 to a catholic mother. She attended a convent school in London, and later studied at Oxford where she rebelled from her strict catholic upbringing and became a feminist.

Narrative

The narrative is about a woman who is distraught that her daughter has run away. She is concerned that her daughter may get into trouble, end up sleeping rough, or even end up going into prostitution.

The girl ran away after an argument with her father, in which he called her a 'dirty slut'. The daughter is depicted favourably at the start with the mother stressing all her positive points. But we learn that she had come home drunk at 3am and has had sex even though she is only 15. She is not perhaps as innocent as her mother wants to believe, but the mother blames her daughter's friends.

The woman reflects on her relationship with her own mother and reveals that she loved her father more than her mother. However, when the woman's mother seemed to favour her granddaughter over her, this upset her. She also reveals that a man called Pete was the love of her life, but he left her so she settled for second best: 'I thought I might as well marry your father'.

The story ends with the mother's protestations about how much she loves her daughter.

Setting

The story takes place in the daughter's bedroom. It becomes a haven for the woman to think about her relationship with her daughter. The action takes place in her mind as she reflects on what has happened and examines the relationships that she has had in her life.

The setting for the arguments was in the family home. This story illustrates the fact that the family home is not always a happy place.

Narrative Structure

At the beginning, the reader might think that the woman is talking about a lover, or husband, who has gone. She seems to be writing a letter that she will never send and her grief is evident. She is curled up on a bed in the dark. She is not eating and takes refuge in a pair of the lost person's unworn shoes. Her grief gives way to anger as the story progresses and she starts to criticise the younger generation. Throughout the text, the woman alternates between tenderness, hurt and concern for her daughter, and anger. She says that the girl is kind and trusting but there is also an undercurrent of anger. The two feelings are juxtaposed throughout.

The text ends with the woman's exclamations of love for her daughter, intermingled with the sad memory that her own mother had never rocked her when she was young.

Themes

- Family relationships.
- Changing relationships.
- Different generations: how the older generation is regarded by the younger generations and vice versa.
- Love and jealousy.
- Growing up.
- Unhappiness: the mother desperately misses her daughter and wants her to come home.
- How past relationships can affect and influence present relationships.
- Things not being what they seem: how the mother perceived her daughter, as opposed to the reality.

Characters

The **unnamed girl** is representative of some girls her age (there is no need for her to be named). She is a rebellious teenager who drinks, smokes pot, stays out late and has underage sex. She is rude to her father. Her mother and grandmother adored her, even though she can be ungrateful and unkind (lines 160–162). At some point she has accused her mother of not wanting or loving her (line 142).

The **mother** (the narrator) is distraught with grief, but is also angry and reflective. She reflects on her own life: she is very aware of her own mother's rejection of her and feels that her mother resented her for getting an education. (She emphasises her education and her good job perhaps to reveal her dislike of her mother.) She says her mother 'looked a bit of a tart', which implies embarrassment or jealousy. She was devastated when Pete left her and is very concerned with what people think about her – when she talks about people who have phoned to see how she is, she imagines them gloating.

She has been scarred by her relationship with her own mother. However, there are indications in the text that she found it hard looking after her own daughter when she was a baby (lines 146–148). She also refers to her daughter as 'an empty-headed blonde'. This is a derogatory description for a mother to apply to her daughter. It suggests that the woman feels that her earlier childhood has been repeated. The woman's mother was a bit of a rebel, just like her daughter.

The **father** is depicted as being very strict. His harsh words have caused his daughter to run away. However, it is implied that he had his wife's support during their arguments. He was not his wife's first choice of husband, but he is 'a good husband, a good father'. Like many fathers, he has found it hard to accept that his daughter is growing up.

Structure and Style

- A **cyclical structure** is created (i.e. the story goes round in a circle): the story suggests that a negative relationship between mother and daughter can be repeated.
- **Short dramatic sentences** (e.g. 'I'm a failure as a mother') highlight parts of the story to shock the reader and stress the woman's erratic thoughts.
- The **first person** is used, like in a **dramatic monologue** but the thoughts are those that would be put into a letter, not spoken aloud.
- The past and present, the different relationships, and the mother's conflicting reactions to her daughter are **juxtaposed** throughout the text.

- **Interrogatives** (**rhetorical questions**) are put to the daughter throughout the text, as the woman questions why her daughter has run away.
- **Informal diction** makes the language conversational, and highlights the family relationship.
- **Extended imagery** – the **metaphor** of the shoes representing the girl. They are cuddled and adored, but most importantly 'they are perfect because they are new, they've never been worn'. The woman likens them to her daughter, wishing that her daughter was still young and innocent.

Exam Preparation

Write down the positive words and phrases and the negative criticisms that the mother applies to her daughter in this story. Of which are there the most?

Growing Up Joyce Cary

The Author

Joyce Cary (1888–1957) was born into an Anglo-Irish family in Londonderry, Northern Ireland. He served in the Red Cross in the Balkan War before settling in Oxford and becoming a professional writer.

Narrative

The story is about a father's relationship with his daughters, who are growing up. He returns home from a business trip eager to see them, but is disappointed to realise that he is no longer the centre of their world and that they are growing up. He is shocked by an incident where they cruelly taunt and chase the beloved family pet, and then attack him (the father), even though it is only a game.

Setting

The story is set in the house and garden of the Quick family. They are a middle-class family who live in a nice neighbourhood, which is implied through the mention of the father's job, his wife's interests and the neighbours' gardens: 'shaved grass and combed beds'. The Quicks' garden is unkempt and unruly – like the young girls.

When the father is desperate for escape he heads for the local men's club. Being away from the family home symbolises being away from the pressures and responsibilities it represents.

Narrative Structure

The story begins by stressing the man's enthusiasm at the prospect of seeing his daughters: he 'looked forward eagerly to their greeting'. He recalls how the girls used to wait at the corner of the road to welcome him home, and he has held on to these memories.

The writer then describes the wild garden that has become the children's domain, as neither of the parents enjoys gardening.

Lines 20–21 are full of positive diction which reflects how the man is feeling at the prospect of seeing his daughters. But, he is disappointed when he sees them as they are both absorbed with their own tasks and barely even register his arrival. There is a great contrast between the greeting that he was expecting and the one he receives. He reflects on the fact that the girls are growing up and he is 'amused at his own disappointment' at their lack of reaction to him.

He watches the children from his deck-chair and is shocked by the violence that he witnesses towards the family dog. The girls then go for their father: 'It seemed to him that both the children, usually so gentle, so affectionate, had gone completely mad, vindictive'.

These scenes contrast with the serenity of the earlier scenes. The man finds himself 'in a mood of disgust', which also contrasts with his earlier mood. He goes to the club and decides to come home only after the children have gone to bed. This contrasts greatly with his earlier enthusiasm to get home and see them.

The story ends with the man accepting, 'She's growing up – and so am I'.

Themes

- Childhood and growing up.
- Different generations: how the older generation is regarded by the younger generation and vice versa.
- Family relationships.
- Unhappiness: the man is unhappy that his relationship with his daughters is changing.
- Things not being as they seem: what the man expected to find when he got home in contrast to the reality.
- The cruel side of human nature – the girls' treatment of their pet dog (and their father).
- Changing relationships.

Characters

The **father**, **Robert Quick**, appears to have the traditional role in the family as the breadwinner. He has traditional views and is shocked when he realises that his daughters are no longer the sweet little girls they once were. However, he is a realist and he accepts change – he recognises that boys will soon come calling for his daughters and he will be regarded as old and stuffy. At the end of the story he accepts that he has changed too.

Both the **daughters**, **Jenny** and **Kate**, are wild and excitable – like the garden which 'belonged to the children'. They are tomboys – happy to be muddy and tousled. They are described as 'naturally impulsive and affectionate' by their father.

The youngest daughter, Jenny, seems indifferent to her father when he first arrives home, but she shows her sensitive side when she nurses her father's wound. She is perceptive because she also realises that her relationship with her father has changed (line 176). Jenny initiates the rough treatment of the dog but Kate soon joins in. The narrator states, 'The sisters adored each other and one always came to the other's help'. Kate initiates the attack on her father.

Mrs Quick is alluded to in the story. She is not at home when her husband arrives, which suggests that she is a very busy woman who, perhaps, does not have a very good relationship with her husband. We are told that 'Mrs Quick was too busy with family, council and parish affairs'. She is amused by the incident. She is preoccupied by her committee business and does not pay her husband much attention. Neither she nor the girls show him much respect.

Structure and Style

- There is a great **contrast** from the father regarding the children as a 'pleasure', to him regarding them as 'mad, vindictive'.
- The **short dramatic sentence** 'Robert was shocked' indicates a pivotal point of change in his feelings towards his daughters.
- The story **describes** places and feelings very well through excellent use of **adjectives**.
- There is a lot of **positive diction** in the opening paragraphs (paragraph starting line 20), which reflects the man's positive feelings.
- **Tone** and **mood** change throughout the story, reflecting the characters' feelings and moods, particularly around line 70 where **images of violence** start to seep into the text, e.g. 'Kill him – scalp him. Torture him.' (line 91).
- Use of **direct speech** helps to portray the relationships between family members (around lines 121–128).
- The wild, unkempt garden **symbolises** the daughters' personalities.

The End of Something
Ernest Hemingway

The Author

Ernest Hemingway was born in 1899 in Illinois, America and worked for a voluntary ambulance service during the First World War. He later became a writer, often writing about ordinary people and the modern world. In 1961 he committed suicide after suffering from depression.

Narrative

This story is about the relationship between a man and a woman living in a town whose main industry has recently collapsed.

The narrative starts by describing how Hortons Bay used to be a thriving mill town, but that all changed when the mill was closed down.

We are then introduced to the couple, Marjorie and Nick. They are fishing together and their fishing is described in great detail, perhaps to illustrate that they are more interested in fishing than they are in each other.

Nick and Marjorie land the boat and start to prepare supper, but there is no physical or emotional closeness between the two. Nick says, 'It isn't fun any more'. The reader is not sure whether he is referring to the fishing or to their relationship, but it later becomes apparent that he is referring to their relationship. When Bill arrives, Nick rejects him too.

Setting

The story is set in Hortons Bay, a deserted old mill town and the lake beside it. The relationship of the couple is over and washed up, just like the old town.

Narrative Structure

The opening of the story is mostly descriptive. It describes the mill as the most important thing in Hortons Bay. One day, the mill ceases operations and all the lumber and machinery are taken away.

The story then goes on to describe the relationship between Nick and Marjorie coming to an end. The fishing is described in great detail, but the exchanges between the characters are short and direct.

Lines 74–106 comprise a lot of direct speech as the relationship between the characters is scrutinised.

The story ends with the decline of the couple's relationship. This reflects the beginning of the story which talks about the decline of the mill and the town.

Themes

- Change: nothing endures except nature / the natural order.
- Changing relationships.
- Love.
- Incompatibility and growing apart – the characters are not compatible any more.
- Unhappiness: the couple is unhappy together.
- Things not being what they seem: what we expect from relationships (Nick expects fun) compared to the reality.

Characters

Marjorie is imaginative – she thinks the mill looks like a castle. She loves fishing, especially with her partner, Nick. Nick gets annoyed because Marjorie knows 'everything', and she knows that she does. She is strong; after being rejected by Nick, she tells him she is taking the boat and rows herself away without making any fuss.

Nick appears remote and cold. He criticises Marjorie by picking an argument with her and telling her that she always knows everything (despite the fact that he was being knowledgeable and telling her what to do earlier on in lines 37, 44 and 52). He then states directly that love is not fun any more. He does not try to stop her when she goes off in the boat. He even rejects Bill's concern at the end of the story and we are then told that 'Bill didn't touch him, either', which highlights Nick's coldness.

It is the characters' relationship, as much as the characters themselves, which is scrutinised in the story.

Structure and Style

- The story has a **circular structure** – it begins by describing the decline of the town and ends by describing the decline of the couple's relationship.
- The **title**, *The End of Something*, has **multiple meanings**: it refers to the end of the mill, the end of the town of Hortons Bay, the end of the couple's relationship, and the end of love.
- The story is **impersonal** – the **third person** is used and the characters' feelings are not described.
- **Short simple sentences**, e.g. 'Nick said nothing', 'It isn't fun any more' suggest a lack of interest between the characters.
- The story contains a lot of **direct speech**, with short sentences and brief conversations. This represents the normality of their relationship – it is nothing special and there is no warmth or intimacy.
- The decline of Hortons Bay **symbolises** the decline of the relationship between Nick and Marjorie.
- Detailed **descriptions** of the mill and the fishing trip are given. However, the characters and their feelings are not described in detail. Line 65 opens a very descriptive paragraph which reminds us that nature prevails, whilst other things change.

Exam Preparation

Choose three of the short stories and write down the settings in each. Alongside, write down how each setting might reflect the plot, the themes or the characters in the story, in some way.

Chemistry Graham Swift

The Author

Graham Swift was born in London in 1949. He studied at both Cambridge and York universities. Much of his writing is about ordinary people dealing with relationships, family and death.

Narrative

Chemistry depicts the relationships between a young boy, his mother, his grandfather and the mother's partner, following the death of the boy's father when he was seven years old. The boy is very close to his grandfather, who assumes the role of the father in his, and his mother's, lives. When his mother's new partner, Ralph, moves in, the boy resents the intrusion into their lives as the family dynamic changes.

The story begins with the boy recalling the sailing of his motor launch boat with his grandfather on the park pond. It is a happy time. But, when Ralph arrives, everything changes.

As the story progresses, the relationships between the boy's mother, Ralph and the grandfather worsen and the grandfather retreats to live in his shed where he practises chemistry. The boy takes an acidic substance from the shed, which he plans to throw in Ralph's face so that his mother will stop loving him. Before this occurs, the grandfather commits suicide by taking a poison that he has manufactured himself. The boy, his mother and Ralph then move house.

At the end of the story, the boy is at the park and he has a vision of his grandfather reaching out to him.

Setting

The pond at the beginning of the story is also a metaphor for life: the boy stands at one side of the pond as he is at the beginning of his life and his grandfather stands at the other, as he is at the end.

The house was originally the boy's grandfather's house and it becomes a place of confrontation, tension and aggression with the arrival of Ralph. It metaphorically represents the protection that the grandfather has given to the boy and his mother.

The shed is a place of retreat where the grandfather practises chemistry. He moves away from the house at the same time that he is moving away from his daughter and rejecting Ralph. The boy, notably, is welcome in both the house and the shed.

Narrative Structure

The narrative moves in a circle – it begins and ends at the pond. This represents the cyclic nature of life.

The story begins positively by describing the bond between the family members. When the boat sinks, the dynamic between the characters alters.

The story moves back and forward in time and is punctuated by the boy's dreams and the life that his grandfather had had with his grandmother. Death and loss also punctuate the story.

The story ends with the bond between the boy and his grandfather being re-established. As his grandfather stated, 'the elements don't change'. He is describing chemistry here but the sentence also represents one of the themes of the story: people, relationships and life change but the elements of each do not.

Themes

- Childhood and family relationships.
- Changing relationships.
- Male–female relationships.
- Different generations: how the older generation is regarded by the younger generations and vice versa.
- Love, jealousy and being in control.
- Unhappiness.
- How past relationships can affect and influence present relationships.
- Coping with death.

Characters

The **boy** has many losses to face – the deaths of his father, grandmother and grandfather, and the boat which represents the bond between him and his grandfather. The boy is happy until line 89, when his hatred of Ralph starts to show. The boy is inquisitive and is fascinated by his grandfather's experiments. He learns his grandfather's lesson at the end: 'though things change they aren't destroyed'.

The **woman (the boy's mother)** is regarded by the men as a possession. Her father does not allow her to work and she is bullied by Ralph. She appears to be frightened of Ralph and panders to his wishes, cooking his favourite meals and drinking with him at night. She starts to neglect her father. She does not cry at his funeral – perhaps she now feels free. The narrator suggests that she does not feel any guilt over her father's suicide.

The **grandfather** is deeply affected by the loss of his wife. His relationship with his daughter and grandson is all-consuming. He is jealous of Ralph's intrusion into their lives. He becomes angry and provokes Ralph. He retreats into his shed where he practises chemistry. This reminds him that although things change on the outside, underneath they remain the same.

Sympathy for the old man is encouraged by such descriptions as 'Grandfather had shuffled back to the house and slipped in, like a stray cat'. But we must remember that he was always in control of the family and he commits suicide when he is no longer in control.

Ralph is seen only through the boy's eyes. The boy thinks Ralph is greedy, bullying and controlling.

Structure and Style

- This is the longest story in the Anthology and it is divided into separate sections.
- **Circular structure**: the pond is the setting at the beginning and at the end.
- The **first person** is used to reflect back in time. This makes the story very personal.
- The story contains an effective **metaphor** of the boat as the bond that ties the family together.
- Places have a **symbolic significance**, e.g. the shed is a retreat from the house and from life; the pond represents the cyclic nature of life.
- The **juxtaposition** of the past and present shows how the past affects our present and the future.
- Dreams punctuate the text, which highlights how the subconscious mind can affect situations in life.
- **Similes** are used to provide vivid **images** of how the boy sees his grandfather as stifled and vulnerable, e.g. his breath 'like the smoke from a muffled pistol', he looked 'like some torpid, captive animal', 'like a stray cat'.
- The story has a **colloquial tone** and **authorial voice**, e.g. 'You see, he liked his food'.
- **Repetition**, e.g. 'Anything can change'. The grandfather repeats this phrase, perhaps to emphasise the point to the reader.

Exam Preparation

Decide for yourself: is the grandfather a control freak who cannot cope when he loses control of the family, or a sad old man, neglected by his daughter and pushed to commit suicide by the treatment he suffers?

Snowdrops Leslie Norris

The Author

Leslie Norris (1929–2006) was born in Merthyr Tydfil, Wales. His father worked as a miner, and much of Norris's work draws on his traditional Welsh upbringing.

Narrative

The story is about a young boy and his family and the events that take place on one specific day. It is the day that a young man in the village is being buried, as he has been killed in a motorbike accident. He was the boyfriend of the young boy's school teacher and she is deeply affected by his death.

The young boy in the story is oblivious to all that is going on because he has been promised by his school teacher that she will take the class to see some snowdrops. He is very excited because he has never seen a snowdrop before.

The narrative follows a typical school day from the boy's perspective, describing his games, his friendships and the things that he delights in. As he is still a young boy, the simplest of things bring him great pleasure.

The two parts of the story (i.e. the grief and suffering of those who knew the young man who died, and the innocence and obliviousness of the children) run together throughout the narrative.

At the end of the story the boy is disappointed by the snowdrop – he expected it to be something wonderful. His dismay is juxtaposed against his teacher's grief.

Setting

The boy's home represents a typical close-knit family living in a small community. The boy is protected from the outside world and is safe in his family home.

The school and the classroom are places of wonder and excitement for the boy.

The story is set in the month of March, when the weather is very cold.

Narrative Structure

The story starts by describing the boy's excitement about seeing the snowdrops and how he imagines they will look.

The family scene at breakfast time is described intricately as the boy watches his younger brother eat. The warmth inside the family house contrasts with the coldness outside. In the house everybody is safe; outside they are preparing for the funeral and it is a bitterly cold day.

As the story progresses, the setting is the school where the wonders of the boy's day unfold. Lines 74, 79, 84, 98 and 121 all stress the liveliness and wonder that the boy experiences in a typical day, and emphasise the innocence of childhood.

The story moves between the boy's home and the school. It ends outside, where nature is stronger than man: it is cold and the snowdrops battle against the elements. The story conveys the message that we can be protected by our families and absorbed in our childhood perceptions, but at some point we must face up to the outside world and the realities of life.

The walk to see the snowdrops is juxtaposed, and contrasted, with the funeral procession. One walk is to see a wonder of nature and the first signs of life in spring: the other walk is to see the cruelty of life – the death of the young man and the end of a life.

Themes

- Relationships – the boy and his father, the boy and his brother, the boy and his friends, the boy and his teacher, and the teacher and her boyfriend.
- Different generations: how the older generation is regarded by the younger generations.
- Coping with death.
- Childhood and school days.
- Unhappiness: the tragic death of the young man, and the boy's disappointment at the snowdrops.
- Things not being what they seem: the school teacher seemed her usual self, but the children were unaware of the grief she had inside.

Characters

The **boy** is typical of a young school child. He is inquisitive and is fascinated by simple things. He feels protected by his father's 'bigness'. He represents childhood pleasures, innocence and the beginning of life.

The **school teacher (Miss Webster)** is brave throughout the day, but she breaks down as she sees the funeral procession. She keeps her promise to the children to see the snowdrops and continues to teach the class during the day. The children are too young to want to intrude into her inner thoughts.

Structure and Style

- The **title** has significance throughout the story. To the young boy the snowdrop is a thing of wonder. To the reader it represents the fragility of life, and growth and endurance. It fights against the cruel weather to survive, just as we have to fight the problems that life might throw at us and carry on.

- **Short simple sentences** depict childhood perceptions, e.g. 'Edmund was very brave'.
- The **childlike tone** (e.g. 'After play they would surely go to see the flowers') highlights the innocence and obliviousness of the children.
- The story is written from the young boy's perspective – his world is evoked by the **detailed descriptions** of his day: how he watches his brother, the games he plays and his drawing of a robin.
- **Contrast**: 'the miraculous flowers' become a great disappointment. The boy wills them to turn into something wonderful.
- **Cold diction** at the opening of the story sets the scene and emphasises the bitterness of the day.
- The cold weather outside **symbolises** the force of nature and the reality that death can intrude into our lives at any time – the young man was only 20 when he died. The snowdrops cannot withstand the force of nature and neither can we as humans.
- The snowdrop is a **metaphor** for life – the boy perceives it as 'one flake of the falling snow, bitterly frail'.
- The adult world and the child's world are **juxtaposed**, to show how the two co-exist.
- **Similes**, e.g. 'Gerald went whooping up the gravel yard like a released pigeon'. This simile creates an image which is full of life and energy, reflecting the lives of young children.
- Childhood pleasures are stressed through **description** with **positive diction**, e.g. 'The taste was incredibly new and marvellous, filling the whole of his mouth with delight and pleasure'.
- **Battle imagery** describes the snowdrops (e.g. 'gallantly', 'bravely'). This reflects nature's strength.
- **Reality** is portrayed in the last line: 'Miss Webster continued to cry aloud in the midst of the frightened children'.

Exam Preparation

Highlight all the similes you can find in this text. Why have they been used and what images do they create?

Comparing Prose

You must be able to write about the relationships between the short stories and be able to compare and contrast them. This means writing about their similarities and differences so you must know the texts very well. You should be able to compare any of the following:

- **Narrative (content)**: what happens in the stories.
- **Setting**: where and when the events in the stories take place.
- **Themes**: what the stories are about – their subjects/messages.
- **Characters**: the characters in the stories – their attitudes, emotions, reactions, what they represent, etc.
- **Structure and form**: all the Anthology stories are short stories, but think about their structure. Are the stories divided into sections? How is punctuation used? Are the sentences long or short? Think about how the structure of each story relates to the meaning, tone or message it is trying to convey.
- **Language and style**: for example…
    - voice: are the stories written in the first, second or third person? What effect does this have?
    - diction: is the vocabulary formal, informal, colloquial, conversational, etc.? Why? What does this tell you?
    - techniques: how do devices such as alliteration, onomatopoeia and assonance contribute to the effect on the reader? Why have they been used?

The lists on page 31 will help you to see some basic similarities between the texts.

As well as relationships between the texts, the questions may ask you to look at the relationships of people within the texts. You must be able to write about the personalities of the characters in the texts.

The lists on page 31 will help you to see some basic similarities between the texts.

Helpful Hints

If a question asks you about the **characters**, it is asking you to write about what the people in the texts are like – their personalities and qualities, not just what they do in the story. We can tell what characters are like by what they say and do and how the author has written about them.

If a question asks you **how the writer shows particular feelings**, it is asking you to write about the language, style and structure that are used.

If a question asks you about **the interesting use of language** it is asking you to write about how the writer shows or presents something through the use of words, language techniques, etc.

The following list shows some of the themes which are common among the short stories. This list will provide a quick reference when you are looking at themes that a number of the stories share.

- **Family relationships** – *Flight, Superman and Paula Brown's New Snowsuit, Your Shoes, Growing Up* and *Chemistry*.
- **Love and jealousy** – *Flight, Your Shoes* and *Chemistry*.
- **Characters' unhappiness** – *Flight, Superman and Paula Brown's New Snowsuit, Your Shoes, Growing Up, The End of Something, Chemistry* and *Snowdrops*.
- **Different generations and how they view each other** – *Flight, Your Shoes, Growing Up, Chemistry* and *Snowdrops*.
- **Coping with death** – *Chemistry* and *Snowdrops*.
- **Changing relationships** – *Flight, Superman and Paula Brown's New Snowsuit, Your Shoes, Growing Up, The End of Something* and *Chemistry*.
- **Childhood** – *Superman and Paula Brown's New Snowsuit, Growing Up, Chemistry* and *Snowdrops*.
- **Things not being what they seem** – *Superman and Paula Brown's New Snowsuit, Your Shoes, Growing Up, The End of Something* and *Snowdrops*.

The following list describes some common structure and style techniques in the short stories.

- **Use of circular structure** – *Your Shoes, The End of Something* and *Chemistry*.
- **Juxtaposition of two worlds** – *Your Shoes, Chemistry* and *Snowdrops*.
- **Personal, autobiographical stories** – *Superman and Paula Brown's New Snowsuit, Your Shoes* and *Chemistry*.
- **Significant title** – *Flight, Chemistry* and *Snowdrops*.

The following example question will give you an idea of what you may be asked to do.

Q. Compare how the young characters react to death in *Chemistry* and *Snowdrops*.

Compare…
- how the characters react to death
- how the writers show these reactions.

This question asks you for…
- descriptions of how the young characters in *Chemistry* and *Snowdrops* react to death
- explanations and evidence of how the writers use language (style and structure) to communicate these reactions and feelings
- similarities and differences between how the young characters react to death in *Chemistry* and *Snowdrops*
- similarities and differences between how the writers use language to convey these reactions and feelings.

Your answer should include a short introduction which is relevant to the question. You should also mention in the introduction the texts that you will be comparing (even if they are given in the question).

You should then go on to compare the two texts named in your introduction.

You could conclude by giving your overall opinion, e.g. whether the characters in the texts react in similar or very different ways, or whether you think the language techniques used in one text are more effective than the other in conveying a character's reaction.

Exam Preparation

Pick out different pairs of stories and write down the similarities and differences you can see between them. These may be in the themes, setting, structure, etc., or the ways in which language is used (style).

Exam Tips

Before the exam, make sure that you...

- know each story well. Read each story at least five times and make sure you know the meaning of any unfamiliar words
- have annotated the texts well – with your teacher's help
- have made your own observations and highlighted them – the examiner wants to see your thoughts and ideas, not just those of your teacher
- have identified and corrected errors that you frequently make in punctuation, grammar and spelling
- have completed all the 'Exam Preparation' and 'Exam Practice' tasks given in this section of the guide
- have perfected the PEE technique (see page 11)
- are able to write confidently about narrative, settings, themes, characters, style, structure and form.

In the exam, make sure that you...

- are aware of the time: you only have **45 minutes** for section A. It is helpful to spend about 5 minutes planning what you are going to write.
- read the questions carefully: choose one that you fully understand and that you can do well
- annotate / highlight the relevant stories with the question in mind – keep looking back at the question
- use the bullet points in the question to help you to write your answer.

Helpful Hints

Learn the terms for the language techniques listed on pages 8–9 and page 15 – what they describe, why they are used, and how they are spelled.

When you use a quote in your answer, make it clear where the quote begins and ends, by putting inverted commas around it, for example...

The boy sees his grandfather as 'some torpid, captive animal'.

Exam Preparation

Read each story in turn. Once you have read a story, read the notes that you have from studying the story in class and at home. Then read the information given about the story in this revision guide. Try writing as much as you can about each story in note form.

Exam Practice

Answer each of the following exam practice questions in 45 minutes and ask your teacher to grade them. Remember to highlight the key words in the questions, and use the PEE technique in your answers. (See pages 34–35 for an example answer.)

Q. Compare how the changing relationships of a parent and his/her child are shown in *Your Shoes* and one other story.

Compare…
- how the relationships change
- how the writers show that the relationships change.

Q. Compare how childhood is portrayed in *Superman and Paula Brown's New Snowsuit* and *Snowdrops*.

Compare…
- the different childhood experiences
- how the writers portray these experiences of childhood through the way they write.

Q. Compare how the characters deal with death in *Chemistry* and one other story.

Compare…
- how the characters deal with death
- how the writers use language to show how the characters deal with death.

Exam Practice

Log onto the AQA website to find past exam questions. Practise completing them in 45 minutes.

Helpful Hints

Do not decide, before you go into the exam, which particular stories you will write about, as you might find that the question on those particular stories is not the best one for you to answer.

When you are comparing texts, try to write about them simultaneously (at the same time), rather than focusing on one, then the other.

Developing Your Answer

Below is an example answer to the following question:

Q. Compare how childhood is portrayed in *Snowdrops* and *Growing Up*.

Compare…
- the different experiences of childhood
- how the writers portray these experiences of childhood.

Notice how this example answer mentions both of the stories in the introduction, linking them to the theme given in the question. The stories are dealt with simultaneously throughout.

Both stories are mentioned in the introduction →

The theme of childhood is depicted in both 'Snowdrops' and 'Growing Up', but we are presented with different portrayals of it.

In 'Snowdrops' the boy is conveyed as a delightful child: he adores his brother and his friends and family, and delights in the simple pleasures of life. At the beginning of the story he is excited about seeing a snowdrop at school. His anticipation of seeing the snowdrop runs throughout the story. His games with his friends and the jokes he shares with them are depicted to provide a picture of childhood innocence and delight. The boy is fascinated by everything – he is even mesmerised by his sandwiches:

PEE is used

'The taste was incredibly new and marvellous, filling the whole of his mouth with delight and pleasure.'

The positive diction shows how he experiences new and wonderful pleasures. Even his journey to school is a time when, 'almost any adventure could happen'.

Quotes are used as part of PEE to prove the points that are made

In contrast to the boy in 'Snowdrops', the girls in 'Growing Up' are older and far less innocent. They become sulky, just sitting in the garden reading and ignoring their father. As in 'Snowdrops', they still delight in childish games, but their games are not so innocent and harmless: they cruelly attack the family pet, and even their father. Their father realises he is afraid of them:

'It seemed to him that both the children, usually so gentle, so affectionate, had gone completely mad, vindictive.'

Correct language terms are used to make points

The negative diction, 'mad' and 'vindictive', highlights the father's fear and contrasts with the portrayal of the innocent and naïve boy in 'Snowdrops'.

The games described in the stories are very different. In 'Snowdrops', the boy and his friend tie another boy's shoe laces together and play with a scarf. On the other hand, in 'Growing Up', the girls' game is more vicious and is described through war imagery: they 'rushed at the man with the rake carried like a lance'.

Connectives are used to link sentences and paragraphs

The girls' relationship with their father changes in the story because they are growing up. They do not greet him with the enthusiasm that they used to, like the enthusiasm the boy in 'Snowdrops' has. Their sulky behaviour is described when their father arrives. They say hello in a 'faint muffled voice', whereas the boy in 'Snowdrops' 'looked at Miss Webster with gratitude'. The girls' lack of enthusiasm for the simple things in childhood contrasts with the boy's delight in everything.

Quotes are used to prove points

However, we do see the tender side of the girls when they tend their father's wound, but the whole thing makes them laugh. They giggle at their father's expense. He is not part of the laughter but the cause of it. They do not seem to respect their father. They tell him what to do, issuing commands throughout the episode with the plaster. This contrasts with the way that the boy in 'Snowdrops' perceives the adults and behaves towards them. He is well-behaved and respectful and the adults' praise is very important to him. He is 'pleased and surprised' when his picture is pinned on the

Personal opinions are given

Answer the question using the prompts given in the bullet points. But remember, you need to show that you are aware of the characters, setting, themes and style (including structure) in each story.

wall. The majority of his conversations with adults are to ask them questions. He still looks up to them and is directed by them.

Settings are compared → The settings of the two stories are similar as both take place in the homes and gardens of the families. The settings are used to help to show different childhoods. In 'Growing Up', the girls' garden is unkempt and wild, like their behaviour. In 'Snowdrops', the garden where the boy sees the snowdrops is a place of disappointment: he 'felt a slow, sad disappointment'. The alliteration of 's' helps to stress the boy's disappointment at the snowdrops. He learns that things are not always as wonderful as he wants them to be. This is similar to the man and his daughters in 'Growing Up': he realises that his relationship with his daughters has changed. The setting helps to show how relationships with others, and the world, change as we get older.

PEE is used

Quotes are used as part of PEE to prove the points that are made

Themes are compared → The theme of change runs through both stories. Similarly, the theme of how differently adults and children see the world runs through both stories. To the girls in 'Growing Up', their savagery was a game that got out of hand; to their father it was an attack. In 'Snowdrops' the flowers represent a wonderful surprise to the boy, but they represent frailty and the threat of death to the adult world.

Style, use of language, and structure are compared → The way that the writers use language gives us a clear portrayal of childhood. In 'Growing Up', the girls' sullenness is seen in the way they respond to their father: 'She answered only in a faint, muffled voice, 'Hullo Daddy''. This simple, direct speech shows that Jenny cannot be bothered to entertain her father. Their cruelty is seen through the war imagery, 'hurled it… like a spear'. However, their episode ends in 'helpless giggles', reminding us that the girls are still only children. At the end of the story, Jenny 'frowned'. This simple word shows she has realised that their relationship with their father has changed. This contrasts with her earlier fit of giggles.

Correct language terms are used to make points

Connectives are used to link sentences and paragraphs

In 'Snowdrops', the events are seen through the child's eyes, which contrasts with 'Growing Up' in which the events are seen through the adult's eyes. In 'Snowdrops', the descriptions are childlike and simple. For example, when the boy is drawing his robin he observes, 'Sometimes the robin looked like a hunchback'. This simile shows how the boy perceived his drawing. His childlike world is evoked by the language that is used – short, simple sentences and phrases such as, 'Edmund waved his finger like a fat white worm in the middle of his dark hand'.

Quotes are used to prove points

Personal opinions are given

The way that the stories are structured also helps in the writers' portrayal of childhood. Both start off with a character being excited and we then see this excitement being unravelled as the themes of the stories are explored. At the end of both stories, the children are growing up, leaving their childish ways behind them.

Conclusion which includes personal opinions → Although childhood is portrayed very differently in the stories, they are similar in the way they both use the setting to represent the characters' feelings and personalities. Language is used effectively in both stories to portray very different childhoods.

Overview of Section B

Section B of the Exam: Pre-1914 and Post-1914 Poetry

The poetry section of your English Literature exam will test your knowledge of poetry from the English Literature section of the Anthology. This includes both the pre-1914 poetry bank and the poems by the contemporary writers, Seamus Heaney and Gillian Clarke or Carol Ann Duffy and Simon Armitage. This guide covers only the poems by Duffy and Armitage.

You will have one hour to complete Section B. You should spend approximately five minutes preparing what you will write.

You will have to answer one question. You will have three questions to choose from and you should read each question carefully. Make sure you choose a question that you fully understand and that you are confident about answering well.

The Questions

You will have to write about two pre-1914 poems and two post-1914 poems (by Duffy and / or Armitage). The questions usually follow one of these formats:

- The question will be in two parts, (a) and (b). One part will ask you to compare two post-1914 poems from a given list. The other part will ask you to compare two pre-1914 poems on a similar theme, from a given list.

OR

- The question will be in two parts, (a) and (b). One part will ask you to compare a named poem from the pre-1914 poetry bank with a named poem by Duffy or Armitage. The other part will ask you to compare a named poem from the pre-1914 poetry bank with a named poem by Duffy or Armitage on a similar theme.

OR

- The question will offer two lists of poems: List A which contains a selection of poems by Duffy and / or Armitage, and List B which contains a selection of poems from the pre-1914 poetry bank. You will be asked to choose two poems from each list to compare.

Helpful Hint

Read the bullet points in the question carefully. They are there to help you.

The following pages look in detail at each poem from the pre-1914 poetry bank (pages 39–53), each poem by Carol Ann Duffy (pages 57–63) and each poem by Simon Armitage (pages 65–72).

You will have studied the poems thoroughly in class. This section will help you to revise the poems so that you are ready to answer the questions in the exam.

Reading and Analysing Poetry

You may have studied all the poems in the pre-1914 poetry bank or just a selection. Similarly, you may have studied just a selection of the post-1914 poems by Carol Ann Duffy and Simon Armitage. The following pages give an overview of *all* the pre-1914 poems and *all* the poems by Duffy and Armitage.

You will probably have notes in your Anthology that you have made in class with the help of your teacher. Remember that you are not allowed to take notes into the exam, but will be given a clean copy of the Anthology to refer to. So you need to ensure that you know the poems thoroughly. It is important that you spend some time reading and analysing the poems on your own.

You should be able to explain each poem in terms of…
- **content:** what the poem is about
- **themes:** issues the writer wants to highlight and / or wants the reader to think about
- **form and structure:** the way the poem is laid out and arranged; its rhythm and rhyme patterns
- **style:** the way that the writer uses words (diction) in the poem; the words chosen; the language techniques employed; and the effect that they have on the reader (you).

Poetry Terms

You should use the correct terms to help you describe how language is used in a poem. Here is a list of the main terms (see also pages 8–9):

Alliteration: repetition of a sound at the beginning of words.

Antithesis: the linking of contrasting ideas.

Assonance: rhyme of the internal vowel sound.

Contrast: a strong difference between two things.

Dialect: words and grammar (that differ from Standard English) used by a particular group of people.

Enjambment: lines that run on and do not stop at the end.

Iambic pentameter: poetry consisting of ten syllables per line, with alternating stressed and unstressed syllables, (i.e. one unstressed syllable, one stressed syllable, one unstressed syllable, one stressed syllable, etc.).

Imagery: the use of descriptive words to create a picture in the reader's mind.

Juxtaposition: the positioning of contrasting words / phrases / ideas close together for effect.

Metaphor: an image created by referring to something as something else.

Metre: poetic rhythm which is determined by the arrangement of syllables in repeated patterns within a line.

Onomatopoeia: words that sound like their meaning.

Paradox: a statement that is contradictory or seems to be nonsensical, but is true.

Persona: a character adopted by the poet for the purpose of the poem; a speaker who is not the poet.

Personification: giving an object or idea human qualities.

Repetition: words, phrases, sentences or structures which are repeated.

Rhetorical questions: questions that do not require answers; the answer is obvious.

Rhyme: the use of rhyming words to affect the sound pattern. Sound patterns can be regular or irregular.

Rhythm: the beat of the poem.

Simile: a comparison that includes the word 'as' or 'like'.

Standard English: the standard use of English words and grammar.

Symbolism: the use of an object, colour, feeling, etc. to represent something else (often an abstract idea).

Tone: the overall attitude / feel of the poem.

Helpful Hint

You will come across the term 'stanza' a lot. Stanza is another word for verse.

The Pre-1914 Poetry Bank

In the pre-1914 poetry bank section of the Anthology there are 16 poems, written by 13 different poets, including some of the best known and most admired poets in the English language.

The earliest (*Tichborne's Elegy*) was written in 1586 and the latest (*The Man He Killed*) in 1902, so they represent over three hundred years of English poetry. This means they are very different in terms of language and style. Their cultural and historical contexts are also very varied.

The overview of each poem (on the following pages) is divided into four sections: **content; setting and context; themes;** and **structure and style**. Some information about the poet is also given.

Content

Think about what happens in the poem. Some of these poems tell a story, while others are about a person's feelings and thoughts at a certain time. When commenting on a poem that has a lot of 'story', e.g. *My Last Duchess*, you need to show that you have understood what is going on, but avoid simply re-telling the story. Think about who is telling the story and why.

Setting

When considering the setting of a poem think about both **place** and **time**. The place might be named (e.g. *Inversnaid* or *Barnegat*), or you might know it is a certain place from the context (Ithaca is the setting for *Ulysses*, and the Tower of London is the setting for *Tichborne's Elegy*). Think about why the poet has chosen this particular setting. What might it mean to the poet and what does it mean to the reader? Other poems are less precise about their settings, but a sense of place is still very important. Think about the different landscapes described in *The Eagle*, *Sonnet* and *The Little Boy Lost* and *The Little Boy Found*.

Time can be just as important as place. Most of the poems are probably set at about the time when they were written so we can consider them in their historical context. Others are set in a period some time before they were written (e.g. *The Laboratory* and *The Village Schoolmaster*). Think about why the poet has chosen to set a poem in the past. Was he writing about his own past, or drawing on the reader's knowledge of a historical period? Does that period have a particular significance?

Context

It is helpful to think about a poem's historical context. How did attitudes at the time that the poet was writing differ from common attitudes today? What would the poets have assumed that their readers knew? For example, poets such as Ben Jonson would assume that their readers were almost all Christian and had knowledge of the Bible. It can also help to know about social conditions at the time.

You might also look at the poem's **literary context**, considering the poet's other work and the kind of poetry that was popular / fashionable when he wrote. For example, the sonnet was an extremely popular form when Shakespeare wrote *Sonnet 130* and he uses his readers' expectations of a sonnet to delight and amuse them with something different.

Themes

A theme is an idea or subject which runs through the poem. Think about how different poets approach similar themes. What do we learn about their attitudes, ideas and feelings?

Structure and Style

There is a wide variety of styles present in this section. The poems range in form and structure from narrative poems (poems that tell a story) to sonnets, and from simple ballad forms to free verse. Some are divided into stanzas, some rhyme, etc. Why did the poets choose a particular form or structure? How can you connect their choice of form and structure to the content and themes of their poems?

Sometimes the language is the language of a persona. Sometimes the poets use literary devices such as alliteration or repetition for effect. Why? Some poets use a lot of imagery. Think about how their choice of imagery relates to the poem's content and themes.

Helpful Hint

Some of the poems might seem difficult at first, but if you approach them with an open mind and make good use of this revision guide and your notes from class, you will find that you can not only understand them, but also appreciate and even enjoy them.

On My First Sonne — Ben Jonson (1616)

The Poet

Ben Jonson (1572–1637) was born in London and lived most of his life there. As a playwright and poet, he was Shakespeare's greatest rival. His eldest son, Ben, died of the plague in 1603.

Content

The poem is about the death of the poet's son, Ben. The poet says goodbye to the boy, who was only seven when he died. He questions his grief, asking why we mourn people's deaths when the dead (especially those who die young) have escaped from the misery and pain of life. He hopes that his son will rest in peace and vows that in the future he will not become so attached to anything he loves.

Setting and Context

The poem is a very personal one, expressing the poet's feelings and his attempts to come to terms with a tragic event. Child mortality was high in the 17th century. However, that did not make it any easier for a parent to deal with a child's death, as this poem vividly demonstrates. The idea that death leads to a better existence, and that therefore we should not mourn the dead, is a conventional Christian belief that would have been familiar to people at that time.

Themes

- Youth and age, and relationships between parents and children: the relationship is considered from the father's point of view.
- Death and fate: everyone must die, but why must some die so young?
- Love: great love leads to sorrow, despair and pain. Is it better not to love someone so much?

Structure and Style

- This poem is in the form of an **elegy** (i.e. a song or poem of mourning for someone who has died).
- It is written in the **first person** so we can assume that the feelings are the poet's own. He uses the **second person** to address his son.
- The poem is written in **rhyming couplets** (e.g. 'joy' / 'boy'), imposing a pattern on the poem which contains the poet's grief.
- Jonson uses **religious imagery**, for example, 'child of my right hand' might remind us of Jesus seated at the right hand of God. However, this phrase is **ambiguous** as it could just refer to the fact that the boy is legitimate – the son of Jonson and his wife. (It is possible that Jonson had children with other women).
- **Ambiguity** in line 10: it is unclear whether 'Ben Jonson' refers to the poet or his son. Is this deliberate, suggesting they are almost as one?
- The **metaphor**, 'his best piece of poetrie' stresses how he, as a poet, could never hope to create anything as special as his son.
- The **diction** is sometimes religious and accepting, e.g. 'sinne', 'just', but it can also be quite angry, e.g. 'rage', 'miserie'. This reflects his changing mood as he tries to come to terms with his loss.
- In the middle four lines of the poem, the poet's grief seems to be breaking out, as he asks **rhetorical questions**. He calms down again in the last four lines, leaving the sense that, although he accepts his loss, he has been affected by it forever.

The Song of the Old Mother
William Butler Yeats (1899)

The Poet

W. B. Yeats (1865–1939) was born in Dublin but spent most of his childhood in London. His family returned to Ireland when he was about 16 and he went on to become one of Ireland's most celebrated poets and playwrights. He was an Irish nationalist and part of a group of writers and artists who were interested in rediscovering Ireland's heritage and history, and in expressing its spirit through art.

Content

In this poem an old woman describes her daily routine: lighting the fire, cleaning and baking. She complains about the laziness of young people.

Setting and Context

The old woman is probably a countrywoman, perhaps from the west of Ireland. However, this is not made explicit in the poem, so she could be from anywhere. The setting of the poem is the house. The woman appears to be uncomplicated and uneducated without any interests beyond her home. Yeats is giving a 'voice' to the ordinary people of Ireland.

Themes

- Different generations: it is not clear whether the young people referred to are the woman's children. It does not really matter, as her sentiments are very general.
- Age and youth: she is conscious of her old age, and the contrast with youth. The picture painted of old age is negative and rather depressing. Is she envious of the young? Does the behaviour of the young women remind her of her own youth?
- Ordinary lives: she is typical of the millions of people whose lives are ruled by drudgery and routine. While she seems to accept this, it is hard to find anything positive in her acceptance.

Structure and Style

- The title says that this poem is a **song**. This suggests that it is something the old woman repeats often. It also reflects its simplicity.
- It is written in the **first person**, but the title and content tell us that the speaker and the poet are not the same person. The old woman is a **persona**. It is possible that the poet is conveying his own attitude through the persona.
- The poem is in **rhyming couplets** (e.g. 'blow'/'glow'). The regularity of the rhyme and of the **metre** (four stressed syllables in each line) reflect the regularity and simplicity of the woman's life.
- The **diction** is simple and straightforward, reflecting the old woman's character and social status. Most of it is written in everyday language.
- There is some **imagery**: the stars are **personified** – they 'blink' and 'peep'. The final line can be taken both literally (the spark of fire that remains overnight before it is re-lit) and **metaphorically** (the old woman's life).
- The poem is dominated by the **contrast** between the old woman's life of hard work and the young people's idleness and lack of care.

Exam Preparation

All the pre-1914 poems are written by men, but several use a female persona. List these poems and consider whether the poets successfully put themselves in the women's minds. Are these poems very different from those in which the persona is male?

The Affliction of Margaret William Wordsworth (1807)

The Poet

William Wordsworth (1770–1850) was one of the Romantic poets (poets who wrote about nature and about emotions). He lived for most of his life in the English Lake District and was inspired by its beauty and grandeur.

Content

The poem's persona, Margaret, has not heard from her son for seven years and does not know whether he is alive or dead. She says that when he left he was good-looking, well bred, innocent and brave. She reflects that children do not realise how much their mothers suffer. She appeals to her son not to be afraid of returning, even if he has not been successful in his life. She speculates on where he might be and wishes he would come to her as a ghost. She can find no answers and no comfort.

Setting and Context

Margaret is an ordinary mother. The only clue we have about her life is that her son was 'Well born, well bred'. She is tied to her home waiting for him, but her imagination, like her son, travels across the world. Her situation would not have been uncommon in an age when many young men left their homes to seek their fortunes abroad, but had no way of contacting those they had left behind. Wordsworth often wrote about people he had seen or met, whose stories he may have known or may have invented.

Themes

- Sorrow, loneliness and despair: Margaret feels completely alone without her son. She may be perceived by others in her community as a mad woman with an 'affliction' (mental distress).
- Parent and child relationships: not knowing her son's fate is worse than if she knew he were dead. We do not know whether he is unable to communicate with her or if he does not care.
- Ordinary lives: she is representative of mothers whose children have left home.
- God / the supernatural: Margaret seeks comfort from her son's ghost, but it does not appear. She has 'no other earthly friend'. Does this imply that she can only find comfort in God?

Structure and Style

- This poem is written in the **first person**, using a **persona** (Margaret). The poem tells us what Margaret feels. It is possible that the poet is conveying his own thoughts through this persona.
- The **structure** is regular and straightforward. Each stanza comprises four lines of **alternate rhyme**, and a **rhyming triplet**. This regularity could reflect the predictability of Margaret's life.
- The **triplets** make each verse sound as if it has gone on a little too long. This creates a **mood** of helplessness and hopelessness.
- Most of the **diction** is like ordinary speech, but there are some 'poetic' words, e.g. 'beauteous', 'grandeur'. Some words are archaic: 'thou', 'thee'.
- As her imagination starts to run riot, the **imagery** becomes very vivid. She contrasts the freedom of birds ('fowls of Heaven') with the situation of her son, and of all humans. There are three nightmarish visions of her son's possible fate.
- **Religious diction:** her devotion to her son makes her speak of him as if he were Jesus. In line 1 he is called 'my beloved Son' (note the capital letter – her son is always given this capital letter.)

The Little Boy Lost... William Blake (1789)

The Poet

William Blake (1757–1857) lived most of his life in London and, although he struggled to make a living, he was – and is – well known both as a poet and artist. He published his poems himself. He claimed to see visions and is sometimes called a 'visionary' or 'mystic'. Although a lot of his poems appear simple, they can be interpreted in many different ways.

Content

In *The Little Boy Lost* a boy cries out to his father, who is walking away from him. The father disappears into the night.

The Little Boy Found starts with the lost boy crying. God appears to him and takes him to his mother, who has been looking for him.

Setting and Context

These poems are set in dream-like landscapes, although the situation of a little boy getting lost is very real.

The poems first appeared in *Songs of Innocence*, a series of poems written for children. They were later re-issued with Blake's *Songs of Experience*, poems which presented a darker, more complex view of the world.

Themes

- Parent and child relationships: the relationship is seen from the child's point of view. The father seems to have no feelings for him and abandons him. The mother, however, is distressed and tries to find her child. There is a 'second father' in God, who reunites the boy and his mother.
- Unhappiness and despair: both the chid and his mother despair and feel alone. However, they are not really alone as God is taking care of them.
- God / the supernatural: God is a very real presence.
- Nature / landscape: the landscape is mysterious and dream-like (or even nightmarish). The darkness and the mire (bog) are dangerous, while the vapour and light seem almost supernatural.

Structure and Style

- The two poems form a pair. In the first poem the child loses his father, while in the second he finds his mother, so there is **contrast** and **balance** between them. The first poem leaves us with a distressing situation, almost a 'cliff-hanger'. In the second poem God intervenes and puts things right.
- The **structure** is **regular and simple** in four-line stanzas with a strong **rhythm** similar to a nursery rhyme, which fits well with the poems' subject.
- The first stanza of *The Little Boy Lost* is written in the **first person**, as the child appeals to his father making the reader respond to his cries.
- The **language** is simple, with a lot of **everyday, monosyllabic words**, showing that the poem could be read by, or to, children.
- The **imagery** is strange and sometimes disturbing. What is the 'vapour'? What is the 'wand'ring light'? God is described using traditional imagery. He is 'like his father', recalling the Christian idea of God the Father, but he is 'in white', symbolic of purity and innocence. Unlike the 'real' father, he guides the child and unites him with his mother.
- The last two lines are **ambiguous**. Is the dale 'lonely' because the child or the mother is lonely? Who is 'weeping'? The mother, the boy, or both?

Tichborne's Elegy
Charles Tichborne (1586)

The Poet

Charles (or Chidiock) Tichborne (1558–1586) was born in Southampton to a prominent Catholic family. He became involved in a number of conspiracies against Queen Elizabeth l, including the Babington Plot. The aim of this plot was to kill Elizabeth so her cousin, Mary, Queen of Scots, could take the throne. The plot was discovered and in September 1586 Tichborne was captured and imprisoned in the Tower of London. He was then executed.

Content

Tichborne reflects on his short life, and how it is about to end.

Setting and Context

A lot of the power of this poem comes from the fact that it really was written by Tichborne on the night before his execution. He had been tried and condemned to death. Imprisoned in the Tower of London, where high-profile prisoners were kept before their executions, he enclosed this poem in a letter he sent to his wife, Agnes. He was 28 years old.

Themes

- Youth and age: the poet is about to die whilst he is in the prime of his life. His feelings about what he will be missing by dying young contrast with the idea expressed in *On My First Sonne* (see page 39), that those who die young are spared the suffering of the world.
- Death: the poet knows he will be executed. His attitude is ambiguous. There is a tone of regret and sorrow, but also a sense that he accepts his fate.

Structure and Style

- This is a very personal poem, written in the **first person** (and emphasised by the line under the title: 'Written with his own hand in the Tower before his execution'.). Tichborne is communicating his state of mind before his death.
- The poem consists of three stanzas of six lines each. The first four lines in each have **alternate rhyme** and are followed by a **rhyming couplet**. This regularity controls the poet's emotion.

- The poem is written in **iambic pentameters**, a **metre** often said to imitate the heart beat. This could represent Tichborne's heart beat.
- The last line of each stanza is the same (this is called a **refrain**) which underlines the inevitability of what will happen. The heavy, short sound of the **rhymes** with 'done' give a sense of finality.
- The **repetition** of 'my' and 'I' at the beginning of lines reflects the personal nature of the poem.
- The poem consists of a series of **paradoxes**, reflecting the central paradox of being young, healthy and lively, yet knowing you are about to die.
- **Imagery** is used to express this contradiction, comparing his situation, for example, to a useless crop (line 3), a day with no sun (line 5), and autumn in the middle of summer (line 8).

Exam Preparation

Identify other poems in this section in which the theme is death. Who has died or will soon die? What is the poet's relationship to that person?

The Man He Killed Thomas Hardy (1902)

The Poet

Thomas Hardy (1840–1928) was a novelist and short-story writer as well as a poet. He was born, and died, in Dorset in South West England. He set most of his work in a historical county of England called Wessex. His characters were inspired by the poor and working-class people of the countryside where he lived.

Content

The narrator of the poem tells the story of his experience as a soldier. He found himself face-to-face with an enemy soldier. They shot at the same time and the other man was killed. He wonders if the man he killed joined up for the same reason as him – because he was out of work. He remarks that if they had met in any other circumstances, they would probably have sat down and had a drink together.

Setting and Context

The poem has a rural setting (shown by the reference 1 'traps' (laid by poachers or gamekeepers to catch wild animals)) and was written when Britain was fighting in the Second Boer War in South Africa. It was a time of high unemployment in England. However, the events in the poem could be taking place anywhere at any time.

Themes

- War and violence: the futility of war. The speaker tells us nothing about who is fighting whom or why. He m... know nothing about the politics behind the war. He certainly did not join up for idealistic or patriotic reasons.
- Death: death is random and without reason. There was no hatred for the other man and he does not know why either of them should have died.
- Ordinary lives: Hardy gives a voice to the working class. The speaker is an ordinary, honest man who sociable and likes a drink. He and the man he killed are victims of a society where they have no power. Unemployment forced them to go to war.

Structure and Style

- This poem tells a **story**; this is reflected in the poem's **form**. There are five stanzas, each with four short lines. In the first stanza the speaker tells us of a meeting with a man. The second reveals that he killed the man, which is quite shocking after the light-hearted first stanza. In the third, he explains why he killed him (the 'official' reason).
- The poem is written in the **first person**. It is in inverted commas, or speech marks, showing that this is not the poet's own voice, but that of a character that he has met or invented.
- The **diction** is **simple** and **colloquial**. He uses non-standard words like 'nipperkin' (a drink) and 'list' (shortened form of 'enlist').
- The **punctuation** makes the poem seem chatty. Exclamation marks and dashes break up the verse, showing that the persona is speaking **informally**. The dashes in the fourth stanza show that he has not planned what he is going to say.
- **Repetition** of 'because' suggests that the speaker is finding it hard to explain why he killed the man.
- **Enjambment** from line 12 leads us straight into the fourth stanza in which the speaker wonders who the man was. In the final stanza, he makes a general remark about war, based on his own experience.

Patrolling Barnegat Walt Whitman (1856)

The Poet

Walt Whitman (1819–1892) was one of America's most influential poets. He believed in the strength of the human spirit as well as the power of nature, and saw America as a place that could change the world. His political views included opposition to slavery and support for free trade. He wrote free verse, rebelling against European 'rules' about rhythm and metre.

Content

There is a storm at sea, which is seen and heard from the shore. A wrecked ship and distress signal are spotted. Some 'weird forms' are seen – perhaps they are people struggling to the shore.

Setting and Context

Barnegat is on the coast of New Jersey, America, so the powerful, dangerous sea is the Atlantic. The title suggests that someone (perhaps the poet) is 'patrolling' the beach (i.e. trying to protect or supervise it). He could be doing this in an official capacity, perhaps as a coastguard.

Themes

- Nature: the seascape is described as wild and threatening using mystic, religious terms.
- Power of man and nature: at first man seems powerless and insignificant in this setting, but do the struggling forms suggest that humans can survive and overcome the power of nature?
- God and the supernatural: the storm is likened to a supernatural being.

Structure and Style

- The lack of a strong **rhythm** suggests that nature is wild – it is fighting against, and escaping from, the poet who is trying to describe it.
- The poem could be said to be **impressionistic**, as it gives a series of impressions of the sea and the land.
- The poet is absent from the poem except for the line in brackets (line 9) where he sees something and questions what it is. The line is broken up, which conveys his excitement.
- The **punctuation** and **syntax** are unusual. At first sight the poem seems to be one, very long sentence. However, it does not contain a main verb. Instead, every line ends with a **present participle** ('-ing'), which gives a sense of speed and movement.
- The way in which the poet switches between aspects of the storm (thunder, wind, waves, snow) adds to the sense of movement and change.
- A **metaphor** describes the thunder: 'demoniac laughter'.
- All aspects of the storm are **personified**: the 'death-wind… watchful and firm advancing'; the beach 'tireless'; the waves 'careering'.
- **Alliteration**, especially of 's', implies the storm's ferocity and stresses that nature cannot be controlled.
- **Imagery** suggests that the storm is supernatural or god-like, but this god is not helpful or caring. The 'savagest trinity' of waves, air and midnight (line 4) is an evil version of the Christian Holy Trinity.
- The last line is shorter than the others. Maybe this shows that the storm has stopped, having run its course. Or maybe the 'savage trinity' (group of three) has allowed the people to reach shore.

Sonnet 130 William Shakespeare (1609)

The Poet

William Shakespeare (1564–1616) is widely thought of as the greatest English writer who ever lived. He was born, and died, in Stratford-upon-Avon, but spent most of his life in London. He wrote a number of plays and long poems, and over a hundred sonnets. Many of his poems seem to be addressed to the same woman, a 'dark lady', about whose identity there have been many theories.

Content

The poet describes his 'mistress'. He compares her looks and behaviour unfavourably to a variety of things. In the end, however, he says that she is as good as any woman who has been flattered with false comparisons.

Setting and Context

A sonnet is a love poem usually addressed to the person whom the poet loved. This form was fashionable in Elizabethan England. Shakespeare kept to the 14-line form, but changed the rhyme scheme.

Themes

- Love: the poem gives an unusual view of love. At first it seems that Shakespeare is insulting his 'mistress', but at the end he states that his is real love which does not rely on false comparisons.

- Art and life / reality: the poem implicitly criticises the work of other poets. He is describing the reality: a real woman, not a fantasy figure.

Structure and Style

- Unusually for a love poem, this **sonnet** is written in the **third person**, describing the loved one rather than talking directly to her. This gives a sense of distance.
- Like all Shakespearean sonnets, the poem consists of 14 lines, arranged into three **quatrains** (i.e. four lines of alternate rhymes), followed by a single **rhyming couplet**. The quatrains make a series of unfavourable comparisons, but the couplet reveals what the poet really thinks. It is as if Shakespeare is playing a trick on the reader.
- The poem is written in **iambic pentameters**, a metre which is said to imitate the heart beat.
- Shakespeare uses the sort of **imagery** that we might expect in a love poem, e.g. he compares the woman's looks to nature (the sun, coral, roses). These images are so common in poetry that they have become clichés. But the fact that he compares the woman to them unfavourably makes them unique.
- The **description** of the woman is very unflattering, e.g. saying that her breath 'reeks' (meaning that it stinks).
- The final couplet completely changes the **mood** of the poem. Is Shakespeare's poem, because of its honesty, more sincere than other love poems which flatter their subjects?

My Last Duchess Robert Browning (1845)

The Poet

Robert Browning (1812–1889) spent his youth travelling and writing. In 1846 he eloped with fellow poet Elizabeth Barrett. For 15 years they lived in Italy. When she died in 1861, he returned to England, becoming very successful and internationally famous.

Content

The Duke of Ferrara is showing off his palace to an envoy (representative) of a Count, whose daughter the Duke wants to marry. He describes a picture of his 'last Duchess' and tells the envoy that she was too free and easy with her affections, so he gave orders to have her 'smiles stopped' (we can presume he had her killed).

Setting and Context

The single word 'Ferrara' after the title refers to both the place and the speaker. Ferrara is a city in Italy and the speaker (the Duke) was inspired by Alfonso II, who ruled Ferrara from 1559 to 1597, at the height of the Renaissance (the period when some of Europe's greatest buildings, paintings and sculptures were created). Artists were usually employed by princes and noblemen. In 1558, the real Duke married Lucrezia, a member of the rich and powerful Medici family (he gave her a 'nine-hundred years-old name' and she brought him money). She died three years later in suspicious circumstances. In 1565 he married Barbara of Innsbruck, who might be the daughter of the Count mentioned in the poem. The poet used the facts he knew about the Duke to create a story of power, jealousy and murder.

Themes

- Jealousy, power and violence: the possessive Duke saw his wife with other men and became jealous. There is no evidence that she did anything wrong. He is a powerful man who wants to control everyone. He is happier with a painting of the woman, than the woman herself.
- Love and death: the Duke had a kind of twisted love for his wife, which caused him to kill her.
- Art: the difference between art and life.
- The human mind: the poet explores the character of the Duke. What turns a man into a murderer?
- History: the poet explores history by imagining the lives of historical figures. The Renaissance was not just a golden age of beauty and riches; beneath the beauty there was corruption and death.

Structure and Style

- Written in the **first person**, this poem is a **dramatic monologue** from the persona's point of view. The Duke's character and motivation can be inferred from what he says.
- We are aware of the listener's presence through **questions** and the use of the **second person**.
- The poem is written in **iambic pentameters**. The regularity of the **metre** and of the **rhyme** (**rhyming couplets**) reflects the Duke's calmness and control in speaking of his violent acts.
- The **diction is informal**. He quotes what other people have said and the lines are broken up by dashes and other **punctuation** marks. This makes him sound casual and almost friendly.
- The painting, covered by a curtain which only the Duke can draw, is **symbolic** of his desire to control his wife.
- The statue of Neptune, 'cast in bronze', represents a powerful male figure taming a wild creature, and might indicate that his next wife will be treated similarly.

The Laboratory Robert Browning (1845)

Setting and Context

The poem is set in France in the 18th century, in a laboratory where poisons are made. 'Ancien régime' i French for 'old rule / government' and refers to the French monarchy just before the French Revolution. The Court of the Kings of France was known for its extravagance, pursuit of pleasure, and corruption. As in *My Last Duchess*, Browning is writing about a historical period before his own. The persona is probably not based on one historical figure, but clues in the poem suggest that she is an aristocrat.

Themes

- Love and death: love and death are entwined. It is the woman's love for the man who rejects her tha leads her to want to kill.
- Jealousy: she is driven to kill by jealousy.
- Power and violence: having an instrument of deatl will give her power over others.
- The human mind: what makes a person a killer?
- History: beneath the glamour of the Court lie corruption and death. The poet and the readers know that the 'ancien régime' was overthrown.

Structure and Style

- The poem is a **dramatic monologue**, written in the **first person**. The poet adopts the persona of someone far removed from him so he can explore her thoughts and feelings.
- We are aware of a listener (the apothecary). We are not given his reactions directly, but in lines 13 and 41 the woman repeats what he has said.
- The poem is in 12 numbered stanzas. This gives the sense of a story and time passing. Sometimes the woman's thoughts seem logical; sometimes she seems to say whatever pops into her head.
- The poem has a quick **rhythm** and a regular **rhyme scheme** (a–a–b–b). It sounds almost frivolous, whicl **contrasts** with the serious subject. This might refle the speaker's nervousness, her frivolous nature (her life seems to revolve around dancing at the Court) c her pleasure in the crime she is about to commit.
- The use of **alliteration** adds to the frivolous tone ('pound at thy powder', 'delicate droplet', etc.).
- There is a **contrast** between the luxury of Court (jewels, fans, etc.) and the laboratory, but the speaker describes the poisons as if she were describing jewels: 'exquisite blue', 'delicate droplet'

The Poet

See page 47.

Content

The poem opens with the woman putting on a mask to protect her from the fumes, which are produced as an apothecary (chemist) makes up a poison for her. She plans to kill her partner's mistress (referred to as 'she' and 'her' throughout the poem). She pictures her partner and his mistress both laughing at her. She asks questions about the poison and imagines the power that she would have carrying it around with her. She starts to imagine killing other women with the poison – Pauline and Elise. However, when the poison has been made she seems disappointed.

She wishes she could have killed her rival instantly when she saw her on the previous night. But she also wants her to suffer.

She rewards the apothecary with all her jewels and a kiss. She looks forward to returning to the Court to dance and, presumably, to kill.

Ulysses Alfred Tennyson (1842)

The Poet

Alfred Tennyson (1809–1892) was one of the most popular poets of the Victorian age. Born in Lincolnshire, he went to Cambridge University but returned home when his father died. He became a successful poet in the 1840s. He became Poet Laureate and was admired by Queen Victoria and Prince Albert. He was the first poet to be made a peer and is often referred to as 'Alfred, Lord Tennyson'.

Content

Ulysses (a king) is bored, and reflecting on his past makes him want to experience new things and go travelling again. He feels that his son, Telemachus, would make a better ruler than him. He speaks to his loyal sailors and urges them to join him in sailing westward, beyond the limits of the known world.

Setting and Context

Ulysses is the Latin name for 'Odysseus', the mythical Greek hero, whose story was told by the ancient Greek poet Homer in the poem *The Odyssey*. Ulysses (Odysseus), after fighting in the ten-year Trojan War, spent many years wandering around the Mediterranean. The poem ends with his return to Ithaca (a small Greek island) to his wife, Penelope, and his son, Telemachus. Many years later, the Italian poet Dante wrote about Odysseus's (Ulysses') 'last voyage'. The ancient Greeks did not know what lay beyond the Mediterranean to the West; it was sometimes thought to be where good people went when they died.

Themes

- Youth and age: Ulysses has experienced many things, but is not ready to settle into a dull, honourable old age. He thinks his son is much better suited to the role of king than he is. Ulysses takes the young man's role of the adventurer.
- Death and fate: the poem could be about accepting death. Ulysses thinks he might meet his old friend Achilles, who died years before, in the 'Happy Isles'. Ulysses embraces life but also accepts his fate and his death.
- The human mind: like Browning, Tennyson uses the dramatic monologue to explore another mind. He explores the 'real man' behind the legendary figure of Ulysses.

Structure and Style

- This is a **dramatic monologue**, written in the **first person** from the point of view of the persona, Ulysses.
- The poem is written in **blank verse** (**iambic pentameters** with **no rhymes**).
- It is in four unequal stanzas. The first tells us about Ulysses's situation. In the second, he explains his feelings. In the third, he talks about Telemachus. In the final stanza, he rallies the sailors to follow him.
- As the poem progresses, Ulysses's **mood** changes from boredom and discontent to enthusiasm and determination.
- His delight in travel and adventure is expressed in the **imagery** used to describe his experiences. He speaks of his 'hungry heart' and his 'drunk delight'. He wants to 'shine' rather than 'rust'.
- The poem uses **antithesis**, **lists** and **repetition** to emphasise certain points.
- The last section of the poem is constructed like a speech, building up to an inspirational rallying cry: 'To strive, to seek, to find, and not to yield'.

The Village Schoolmaster Oliver Goldsmith (1770)

The Poet

Oliver Goldsmith (1728–1774), the son of a clergyman, was brought up in rural Ireland. He went to Trinity College, Dublin, before travelling around Europe, eventually settling in London. He was poor for most of his life, but found success with a comedy play, and a long poem, *The Deserted Village*, from which *The Village Schoolmaster* is taken.

Content

The poem describes the schoolmaster of a village school. (Goldsmith himself attended a small village school and he could be writing about his own teacher.) The schoolmaster is well known in the village and respected by the children, who know how to read his moods. They sometimes pretend to find his jokes funny and are sometimes afraid of him. His knowledge is vast and he uses it to argue with the parson (vicar), impressing the local people, who are amazed that one person could know so much.

Setting and Context

The poem is set in a village in the mid-18th century. Education was not compulsory until about a hundred years later. The school was probably very small with only one teacher, and children of different ages in one class. It is unlikely that the children attended for long, as they would have had to start work at a very young age. Some never went to school and many adults could not read or write; the schoolmaster and parson were probably the only educated people they ever met.

Themes

- Youth and age: the poet reflects on his childhood. He writes about how children view adults, especially those in authority, and how those adults treat children. The relationship seems warm and positive but formal and distant.
- Ordinary lives: the schoolmaster is not given a name. He is defined by his job and it is this which earns him the respect of the uneducated villagers.
- Education: the poem paints a picture of education and schools in the 18th century.

Structure and Style

- The poem is written in the **first person,** but it is not about the poet himself. The focus is on the schoolmaster. When the poet says 'I knew him well', he is making the schoolmaster seem real.
- The poem is written in **iambic pentameters**, a **metre** which imitates the heart beat. This gives it a smooth, regular feeling which could reflect the regularity and predictability of village life.
- It is in **rhyming couplets**, the simplest of rhyme schemes, which conveys the simplicity of country life. It is also the rhyme scheme most used by children, which reflects the school setting.
- There is a **tone** of nostalgia and amusement. The poet recalls the simplicity and naïvety of those who were in awe of the schoolmaster's knowledge.
- Some of the language, e.g. the **alliteration** of 'learned length', imitates the schoolmaster's own style of speech, which so impressed the villagers.

The Eagle Alfred Tennyson (1851)

The Poet

See page 49.

Content

The poem describes an eagle, perched on a rock and looking down at the sea. Suddenly the eagle swoops down, probably to catch its prey.

Setting and Context

The poem is set in a wild, rugged, hot landscape. There are no humans in the poem.

Themes

- Nature: the eagle represents the beauty, power and violence of nature.
- Power: although there is no human presence, the language and imagery indicate that the poem is also about human power and destructiveness.
- Freedom and wildness: the landscape and the bird are completely wild and untouched by man.

Structure and Style

- The poet is not present in the poem at all. He simply describes the eagle in the **third person**.
- The poem is very short. Each of the two stanzas has only three lines. The impact of this on the reader might reflect the impact of the bird on its prey. The first stanza describes the bird's stillness. In the second stanza the eagle moves and attacks.
- All three lines of each stanza **rhyme**, forming **rhyming triplets**.
- The poet uses **alliteration**: the hard 'c' sounds in the first line give an impression of violence: 'he clasped the crag with crooked hands'.
- The eagle is **personified**, taking on human qualities. He has 'hands' rather than claws, and he 'stands' rather than perches. The sea is also **personified**: it 'crawls'.
- The **imagery** makes the eagle seem like a king or a military leader. The mountains are 'walls' like those of a fortress or castle. He is at the centre of the world ('Ring'd with the azure world') and he looks down on the world. The sea is made to sound old and weak: 'wrinkled', 'crawls'.
- In the last line the poet uses a powerful **simile**: 'like a thunderbolt he falls'. This suggests not only the speed and suddenness of the eagle's movement, but also describes the way in which a bird falls on its prey. The 'thunderbolt' might also make the reader think of Zeus, the most powerful of the Greek Gods, who hurled thunderbolts at his enemies.
- The eagle is **described** in the first stanza as being 'Close to the sun' and at the end he does not swoop or dive, but 'falls' to the sea. This might remind readers of the classical myth of Icarus, who flew too close to the sun and fell into the sea.
- The poem could be seen as a **metaphor** for human power and destruction: how humans may think they are in control of the world, but nature is always stronger. At the end of the poem, 'thunderbolt' is used to remind the reader of nature's overbearing power.

Exam Practice

Compare how nature and the weather are described in this poem and in *Sonnet* by John Clare and *Patrolling Barnegat* by Walt Whitman.

Inversnaid Gerard Manley Hopkins (1881)

The Poet

Gerard Manley Hopkins (1844–1889) was born in Essex. As a young man, he converted to Catholicism and became a Jesuit priest. He destroyed all his poems, thinking that the writing of poetry might not be a suitable occupation for a priest. However, his superiors disagreed and he took up writing again, using his poetry to express his faith. His poems were published after his death.

Content

A burn (stream) falls down into a lake below. The poet describes the foam on the lake, then the landscape through which the stream flows. He finally asks what the world would be without such wild places, and makes a plea for them to remain.

Setting and Context

Inversnaid is in the Scottish Highlands, above Loch Lomond. Hopkins worked as a priest in Glasgow. Although, there is no direct mention of God in the poem, Hopkins saw God in the power and beauty of nature.

Themes

- Nature / landscape: Inversnaid is a wild, untamed landscape. The beauty of nature lies in its wildness and power. The poet recognises the importance of the natural environment.
- Faith and religion: while belief in God is not mentioned as such, despair (which in Catholicism is the result of being cut off from God) is 'drowned' by the stream.

Structure and Style

- There are four stanzas, giving a **logical structure** to the poem. The first stanza describes the burn's journey to the lake, the second the burn meeting the water of the lake and the third the landscape through which it travels. In the fourth stanza, the poet reflects on nature and its importance.
- There is a very strong **rhythm**, based on the natural stresses of speech, which reflects the force of the water.
- **Alliteration** is used to give a sense of the speed and force of the water: 'rollrock… roaring', 'coop… comb', 'fleece… foam', etc.
- **New, made-up words** and original combinations of existing words make us see nature with new eyes, e.g. 'twindles', 'heathpacks', 'pitchblack'.

- **Dialect words** such as 'burn' (stream) and 'braes' (riverbanks) are also used.
- Hopkins uses striking and unusual **metaphors**, as if trying to pin down the nature of the stream by comparing it with everyday things ('horseback brown', 'windpuff-bonnet', 'broth / Of a pool').
- Nature is **personified**: the brook 'treads' and the ash tree is 'beadbonny', as though it is a pretty woman wearing beads.
- A feeling of 'Despair' is also **personified** (and is given a capital letter, relating it to Catholicism). The water 'rounds and rounds Despair', chasing it until it drowns. The water here can be seen as the instrument of God.
- In the final stanza, the poet addresses the reader. He asks a **rhetorical question** (lines 13–14) before making an appeal on behalf of wild nature.
- **Repetition** is used in the final verse to really get the point across.

Exam Preparation

Hopkins and Whitman (page 45) both see the power of the supernatural in nature. How do their attitudes to this presence differ?

Sonnet John Clare (1841)

The Poet

John Clare (1793–1864), the son of a farm labourer, started farm work at the age of 11, going to school in the evenings. He was known as the 'Northamptonshire Peasant Poet': his work reflected life in rural England. He suffered from alcoholism and mental illness, and spent much of his later life in asylums.

Content

In this poem, Clare writes about his love for the countryside, in particular during the summer. He describes the plants and animals that he sees.

Setting and Context

This poem could be set anywhere in the English countryside. Romantic poets used images of the countryside to express their ideas and emotions. Clare also does this, but his view of nature is entirely positive. He strongly believed in the importance of rural life, in man being at one with nature, and in the countryside belonging to everyone, not just powerful landowners.

Themes

- Nature and man's relationship with nature: the poet tells us how much he loves the summer and all the aspects of nature that he sees in that season.
- Love: he is not writing about love for a person, but about his love of nature and the countryside.
- Freedom and innocence: there are no restrictions in the landscape described here, and nothing bad or unpleasant spoils the view.

Structure and Style

- The title says this is a **sonnet**. A sonnet is usually a love poem, addressed to a person, but this poem is about the poet's feelings for a season (summer) and for nature. The fact that the title is simply *Sonnet* emphasises that it is a love poem.
- The poem has 14 lines, following the usual **structure** of a sonnet. However, it is written in **rhyming couplets**, making it much simpler. This reflects the simplicity of the subject matter.
- It is written in the **first person**, indicating that it is an account of the poet's genuine feelings.
- The **repetition** of 'I love' / 'I like' emphasises his love and draws attention to the number and variety of natural things that he loves.

- There is no **punctuation** in the poem. Perhaps this reflects the poet's love of freedom, which he associates with nature, and his opposition to the fencing in and ownership of the countryside.
- **Imagery** is used to compare one thing in nature to another: 'reed clumps rustle like a wind shook wood'. This could suggest that nature is the only thing worthy of comparison.
- **Personification**: the insects' wings are 'happy' as they 'sport', and the beetles 'play'. This gives a sense of childhood innocence and joy.
- The poem is very **visually descriptive**: it uses words which make us think of innocence, richness and brightness: 'white', 'gold', 'clear', 'bright', etc.
- The **diction** is fairly **simple**: the language of ordinary countryman, including **colloquial** names for plants, e.g. 'Mare blobs', 'flag nest', 'hay grass'.

Comparing Pre-1914 Poetry

The examiner wants to see that you can read, understand and comment on poetry. You should be able to see relationships between the poems. You must show that you can compare poems in different ways.

In the exam you will be asked to compare the poems from the pre-1914 poetry bank both to each other, and to poems by Carol Ann Duffy and Simon Armitage. Usually the questions will focus on common themes, so you need to think about how the poems can be linked by theme or subject matter.

This list describes some common themes in the poems from the pre-1914 poetry bank. (Note that they are not the only ones you can compare.)

- **Nature / landscape** – *The Little Boy Lost* and *The Little Boy Found, Patrolling Barnegat, The Eagle, Inversnaid* and *Sonnet.*
- **Parent and child relationships** – *On My First Sonne, The Affliction of Margaret, The Little Boy Lost* and *The Little Boy Found* and *Ulysses.*
- **Youth and age** – *On My First Sonne, The Song of the Old Mother, Tichborne's Elegy, Ulysses* and *The Village Schoolmaster.*
- **Nostalgia / memories** – *On My First Sonne, The Song of the Old Mother, The Affliction of Margaret, Tichborne's Elegy, The Man He Killed, My Last Duchess, Ulysses* and *The Village Schoolmaster.*
- **Ordinary lives** – *The Song of the Old Mother, The Affliction of Margaret, The Man He Killed* and *The Village Schoolmaster.*
- **Death** – *On My First Sonne, The Affliction of Margaret, Tichborne's Elegy, The Man He Killed, My Last Duchess, The Laboratory* and *Ulysses.*
- **Sorrow and despair** – *On My First Sonne, The Affliction of Margaret* and *The Little Boy Lost* and *The Little Boy Found.*
- **God / the supernatural** – *On My First Sonne, The Affliction of Margaret, The Little Boy Lost* and *The Little Boy Found, Patrolling Barnegat, Ulysses* and *Inversnaid.*
- **Love** – *On My First Sonne, Sonnet 130, My Last Duchess, The Laboratory* and *Sonnet.*
- **Violence and power (of man and nature)** – *The Man He Killed, Patrolling Barnegat, My Last Duchess, The Laboratory* and *The Eagle.*
- **History / the past** – *My Last Duchess, The Laboratory, Ulysses* and *The Village Schoolmaster.*

The poems can also be linked by form, structure or style. This list describes some common forms, structures and style techniques in the poems from the pre-1914 poetry bank.

- **Dramatic monologues and poems where the poet adopts a persona** – *The Song of the Old Mother, The Affliction of Margaret, The Man He Killed, My Last Duchess, The Laboratory* and *Ulysses.*
- **Poems in the form of a sonnet** – *Sonnet 130* and *Sonnet.*
- **Poems where nature is personified** – *Patrolling Barnegat, The Eagle, Inversnaid* and *Sonnet.*

See pages 74–75 for comparing the poems from the pre-1914 poetry bank with poems by Duffy and Armitage.

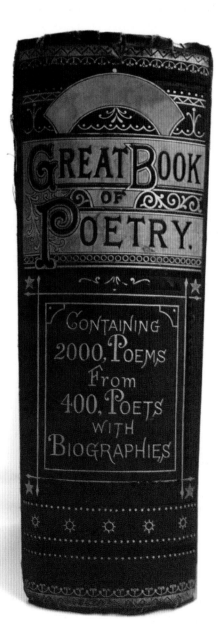

Post-1914 Poetry: Duffy and Armitage

Carol Ann Duffy and Simon Armitage are contemporary poets who deal with issues that are highly relevant to today's society. A number of Duffy's poems feature depressed or disturbed members of society who feel they are ignored and resent the world in which they live, whilst many of Armitage's poems explore relationships and the impact that they have on people's lives.

Whilst we can presume that both Duffy and Armitage are drawing on past experiences in some of their poems, in others they write through personae as a device through which to explore other lifestyles.

The overview of each poem is divided into four sections: **content**; **feelings, characters and relationships**; **themes**; and **structure and style**. However, do not forget to also think about **setting** and **context**.

Content

Think about what happens in the poem. Does the poem tell a story? Or is it a description of a person, place, object or emotion? When commenting on a poem that tells a story, e.g. *Hitcher* by Armitage, you need to show that you have understood the other layers of meaning in the poem, as well as the story on the surface.

The references in these poems are often contemporary, referring to modern creations and trends like 'Batman and Robin' and pierced ears, but the meanings behind these references are often wider reaching.

Feelings, Characters and Relationships

Think about the ways in which relationships are explored in the poem. Look at the emotions conveyed in the poems; many of Duffy's and Armitage's poems are about thoughts and feelings at a certain time and have themes that are relevant to everybody. Look at the characters in the poems; Duffy refers to historical, literary or biblical figures in some of her poems: *Havisham*, *Elvis's Twin Sister*, *Anne Hathaway* and *Salome*.

Themes

A theme is an idea or subject which runs through the poem. You should look for themes and ideas in these poems that connect them to each other, and to poems from the pre-1914 poetry bank.

Think about how different poets write about similar themes. What do we learn about their attitudes and ideas? For example, what does *Those bastards* tell us about Armitage's views towards the rich and the upper classes?

Structure and Style

Although there are only two poets in this section, the variation in style amongst the poems is huge. The poems range in form and structure, and include narrative poems (poems that tell a story), sonnets, structured verse and free verse. Some are divided into stanzas, some rhyme, etc. Why have the poets chosen a particular form or structure? Think about how the choice of form and structure relates to the content and theme of the poems.

Duffy and Armitage use colloquial language in their poetry, but this is part of a highly crafted use of language. The language may be simple but the images and ideas can be complex. Sometimes the language in the poem is in the first person and reflects the words or thoughts of a persona. Sometimes the second or third person is used. Language techniques such as alliteration, onomatopoeia, repetition and imagery are used. Ask yourself how these language techniques relate to the content, themes and tone of the poem. The language that the poets use is crucial to the meanings of the poems.

Setting

When considering the setting of a poem think about both place and time. The place might be named, as in Armitage's *Hitcher*. Think about why the poet has chosen this particular setting. What might it mean to the poet and what does it mean to the reader?

In these poems the events are generally more important than where and when they take place. The absence of a particular setting can suggest that the events could happen anywhere, at any time.

Context

It can be helpful to think about a poem's context. For example, Duffy's *Salome* and *Anne Hathaway* are based on biblical and historical characters, and Duffy's *Havisham* is based on the character Miss Havisham from Charles Dickens' novel *Great Expectations*. These poems are much easier to understand if you are aware of their historical contexts.

Carol Ann Duffy

Carol Ann Duffy

Carol Ann Duffy was born in Glasgow in 1955. She grew up in Staffordshire with her parents and four younger brothers. She attended a Roman Catholic primary school and a convent school before going on to study philosophy at Liverpool University.

Duffy became a poet and playwright and now teaches poetry and creative writing at Manchester Metropolitan University. Her daughter, Ella, was born in 1995.

She has written many poems about children, women, love and desire, memories and death. Duffy's poems are often written from the point of view of a persona. The personae she creates tend to be isolated individuals who feel shut out from society.

Helpful Hint

Duffy's and Armitage's poems tend to use simple, everyday words rather than 'poetic' words. It is the way in which these words are used that makes the poems interesting and open to interpretation.

Havisham Carol Ann Duffy

Content

This poem is about a failed relationship. The woman's lover has left her and she reveals her innermost thoughts and emotions.

The poem's title refers to the spinster in Charles Dickens's novel *Great Expectations*. In the novel, Miss Havisham was stood up on her wedding day and was affected by it so deeply that she kept her wedding dress on for years and kept the wedding cake in her room.

The woman in the poem is based on the character Miss Havisham from the novel. She has been jilted by her lover and is bitter about this fact.

Feelings, Characters and Relationships

Havisham's violent hatred of the man who has left her is portrayed in the first line of the poem. She describes her behaviour when he left her: she spent whole days in bed. She reveals herself as a victim: she wonders who did this to her. She has fitful sleep full of curses and stabs her wedding cake violently. She asks for a corpse for her honeymoon.

She has been destroyed by her love for a man. Her whole life has been affected as is shown by her behaviour and her thought patterns. She has been broken in spirit and in mind. Her love has turned to hatred and she even hates herself.

Themes

- Relationships: Havisham's relationship with her ex-fiancé failed.
- Love and hate: the woman has intense hatred for the man she once loved. She wants to kill him.
- Violence and death: her intense anger causes her to become violent and wish the man dead.
- Memories: the woman vividly remembers the days following the cancelled wedding.

Structure and Style

- The poem is written in the form of a **dramatic monologue:** the writer addresses the reader directly.
- The character is referred to simply as Havisham, without 'Miss'. This could be because she represents all women who have been disappointed in love, rather than one specific character.

- **Angry and violent diction** is used throughout the poem, e.g. 'strangle', 'curses', 'bite', to convey the strength of her anger.
- The use of 'stink' could show that she has been neglecting herself, but it could also represent that, internally, she has become rotten (full of hatred).
- **Onomatopoeia** highlights the power of her anger by appealing to the reader's senses, e.g. 'cawing' makes her screams sound like those of a wild animal or bird.
- She addresses the man with an **oxymoron** at the beginning of the poem. This is a shocking opening line which sets the **tone** for the poem. It shows her divided feelings for him.
- In line 15, the woman's need for revenge is shown by the fact that any man's body will do. This shows her hatred for all men. The use of 'its' in the third stanza suggests that she no longer sees men as human.
- In line 4, the 'ropes' are a **metaphor** for the veins in her hands. This could refer to the appearance of old women's hands which would illustrate how long her grief lasts, or it could refer to her anger, which causes her veins to stand out. She is saying that she could strangle the man with her bare hands.
- The balloon bursting in line 13 could be a **metaphor** for how the woman's dreams of marriage (and her heart) have been broken.
- The final word in the poem is broken to represent the woman's faltering voice and her constant tears.

Elvis's Twin Sister Carol Ann Duffy

Content

The poet imagines that Elvis Presley has a twin sister who is a nun in a convent. (In reality, Elvis did not have a sister.) In contrast to Elvis's life, hers is simple and happy. She is fulfilled and content in what she is doing. Elvis had a tortured life in which he strove to find happiness, but it always seemed to elude him. His sister appears to have found the fulfilment that he desired. She finds pleasure in the simple things like tending the gardens and watching things grow. Unlike her famous brother, she is never lonely. She is not a conventional nun.

Feelings, Characters and Relationships

Elvis's sister uses the same kind of language that Elvis used and 'moves her hips' just like him, but she is very different and her life is contrasted with his throughout the poem. He was lonely and felt that people betrayed him: she is never lonely and is content. He led a tortured life, always looking for happiness: she finds happiness in the simple pleasures of life. He wore ornate outfits; she wears simple clothes. He lived in a mansion called Graceland; she lives in her land of grace (God).

She is emotionally stable and delights in the fact that she is 'alive and well'. Her relationship with God gives her all the emotional fulfilment that she needs in life.

Themes

- Family relationships.
- Finding happiness: happiness comes from within.
- The shallowness of the entertainment industry and the value of living a simple life.

Structure and Style

- The use of the **first person** allows the reader to get involved with the character in the poem and to share her thoughts and emotions.
- The **questions** and statement in italics at the beginning make the reader stop and think, and give an idea of what the poem is about.
- In the third stanza, there are references to singing – peaceful, religious singing – which contrast with the 'rock 'n' roll' style of Elvis's singing.
- **Informal, colloquial language** is used, e.g. 'y'all,' 'lawdy', 'digs'.
- **Juxtaposition** of images from Elvis's life and the simple life of his sister.
- **Contrast** is evident throughout the poem, e.g. the 'simple habit' of the nun contrasts with the ornate clothes Elvis used to wear.
- There are numerous references to Elvis in the poem, e.g. 'blue suede shoes', 'Graceland', 'trademark slow lopsided smile', 'Lonely Street', 'Heartbreak Hotel'.
- **Rhyme** is used irregularly which gives the poem a jaunty feel, reflecting the happy character of the nun and perhaps reflecting music.

Anne Hathaway Carol Ann Duffy

Content

The poem is written from the point of view of Anne Hathaway, William Shakespeare's wife. In his will, Shakespeare gave her his second best bed. The poem deals with her reflections of what they did in this bed.

It is another poem that deals with the story of a famous historical figure. Duffy uses these famous figures to become representative of all people in similar situations.

The poem is written in admiration and respect of Shakespeare as a lover and as a writer.

Feelings, Characters and Relationships

Anne Hathaway is a sensual woman who expresses her sexual feelings. Her adoration of her husband is apparent. She writes in ornate language like her husband. She values his art as a lover and as a writer. She merges the two: 'His touch a verb dancing in the centre of a noun'. Nouns are usually the object done unto by a verb – the sexual and the literary merge in the woman's thoughts.

Themes

- Memories: the persona vividly remembers her time with Shakespeare.
- Love and passion: she describes her love and passion for Shakespeare and also her respect and admiration for him.
- Finding happiness: she found immense happiness with Shakespeare – this is conveyed throughout the poem.

Structure and Style

- The poem is in the **form** of a **sonnet** with the last two lines a **rhyming couplet**. The sonnet was the form most used by Shakespeare in his poetry.
- The references to 'forests, castles, torchlight, clifftops, seas' represent the places Shakespeare wrote about. They also show how Shakespeare's love made Anne feel excited and how she felt that he took her to different places – as in a dream.
- The poem contains some **erotic images**, e.g. 'I dreamed he'd written me, the bed a page beneath his writer's hands'.
- The poem appeals to the reader's senses through the **vivid descriptions** and **comparisons**.

- **Alliteration** of 'living laughing love' stresses her positive feelings.
- She denounces the writers of prose by using 'dribbling' to describe them, the only negative word in the whole poem.
- **Metaphors** and **similes** are used throughout the poem which highlight Anne's intense love for Shakespeare, and her strong memories of him.
- The last two lines are **ambiguous**. A casket can be a case for keeping jewels, or it can be a coffin. So, either Anne's memories of Shakespeare are so precious that she treasures them in her casket, or she is now leading a deathly life without him.
- **Enjambment** represents how her emotions and reflections of her husband flow, and gives energy and liveliness to the feelings expressed.

Salome 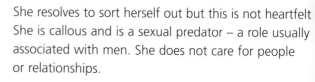 Carol Ann Duffy

Content

Duffy updates the biblical story of Salome, writing from the perspective of a modern-day Salome. Salome was a biblical woman who was a very sexual character. Her stepfather, King Herod, was so captivated by her that he said she could have anything she wanted. She asked for the head of John the Baptist on a platter. This wish was granted.

In this updated story, Salome has woken with a hangover and is reflecting on her sexual conquests. She decides she needs to stop drinking, smoking and having one-night stands. In the final stanza, she pulls back the sheets to reveal that she has cut the man's head off.

Duffy's treatment of a cruel story with some humour is interesting. She fuses the old story and the modern lifestyle together. She could be expressing her belief that people and situations do not really change.

Feelings, Characters and Relationships

Salome reflects on her lifestyle. She is not shy about the fact that she sleeps with different men and she admits that she will do it again in the near future. She lists the men (all are names of Jesus's disciples) but she cannot remember who the man is beside her.

She resolves to sort herself out but this is not heartfelt. She is callous and is a sexual predator – a role usually associated with men. She does not care for people or relationships.

She is wealthy and calls for her maid to bring her food to help with her hangover.

Themes

- Violence and death: the woman sleeps with a man and then kills him.
- Troubled relationships: Salome is a very sexual woman who uses men before killing them.
- Stereotypes: the poem challenges the sexual stereotype of women as subservient and passive, and men as sexual predators.

Structure and Style

- The poem is related to an old biblical story. Perhaps the poet is asking whether people ever really change.
- **Alliteration** gives a casual, jaunty **tone** to the poem.
- A number of **interrogatives** are used as Salome tries to recall who the head beside her is.
- **Colloquial language**, e.g. 'Good-looking, of course'.
- Single words are used for emphasis, e.g. 'strange'.
- **Enjambment** allows her thoughts to flit between the night before and her current hangover.
- **Contrast** of Salome (sexual) with the maid's 'innocent clatter'. This highlights Salome's lack of innocence.
- The man is referred to as a 'beater or biter', which gives a **negative portrayal** of men.
- **Humour** is used in the last lines: 'ain't life a bitch' is followed by the fact that she has beheaded the man.
- **Juxtaposition** of the original story and a real beheading with a metaphorical beheading – the man may have lost his head by having sex with her or she has claimed him as a prize – his head is a trophy (like a 'notch on the bedpost'). The whole poem would then be an **extended metaphor**.

Exam Practice

Compare how the persona in this poem feels about her dead lover with how the persona in *Anne Hathaway* feels about her dead lover.

Before You Were Mine Carol Ann Duffy

Content

The poet considers her mother's life and the fun that her mother would have had before she was born. The poet also thinks about how her mother was treated by her own mother. She remembers the things she did with her mother when she was younger.

Feelings, Characters and Relationships

The relationship between the poet as a girl and her mother was a positive one. However, as the title implies, she regards her mother as her possession. The poem suggests that once a child is born, a woman becomes just a mother rather than a woman in her own right.

When the poet's mother was young she used to have great fun with her friends, laughing and dancing. The emphasis is on the emotions of youthful joy and exuberance, carefree existence and fond memories.

The emotions portrayed are positive but there is a slightly unsure tone to line 11. It is as if the poet wishes she could have shared some of her mother's youth with her.

The poet remembers her mother fondly. Her memories are all positive. However, there is arguably a slightly selfish side to the poet as she wants to have been part of her mother's youth as well as her present day. This helps to convey the idea that children are all-consuming.

Themes

- Memories and happiness: the poet has fond childhood memories.
- Growing up: how women change as they grow up and have children of their own.
- Family relationships: the responsibility that being a parent brings.
- Love: the poet loves her mother and is possessive of her.

Structure and Style

- The poem is written in the **first person**, but the poet addresses her mother directly using the **second person**.
- In the first stanza, the **present tense** and **present participles** are used so the reader can feel the immediacy of the action and feel part of what the writer sees in her mind.

- **Colloquial, everyday language** is used, which conveys the close relationship between parents and children.
- The images **appeal to the senses** (sight and sound) throughout the poem; **onomatopoeia** is used, e.g. in 'clatters' and 'sparkle'.
- **Alliteration**, e.g. in lines 16 and 17, add to the liveliness of the poem.
- The poem is full of **vivid, lively images** of fun times and expressions of affection.
- **Repetition** of the poem's title in the second and last verses stresses the difference in the poet's mother before and after the poet was born.
- The poet **compares** her mother to Marilyn Monroe, i.e. glamourous, attractive and fun.

We Remember Your Childhood Well Carol Ann Duffy

Content

The poem is written from the perspective of parents, who are recalling their child's childhood. We can presume the child is a daughter (but there is no evidence to support this apart from the fact that the personae in Duffy's poems are predominantly female).

There is a debate throughout the poem about the way the child was treated, but her point of view is not heard directly. Her arguments against the points that are made are given through the parents' viewpoint.

We are told that the girl was sent away, but it was disguised as a holiday. The people that she stayed with were 'firm'. This could mean that she was subjected to hard discipline. The parents ascertain that everything they did was for the best.

Feelings, Characters and Relationships

The relationship between the child and her parents is not good, and it appears it never was. The child's viewpoint is that her parents used to argue all night and keep her in. She wasn't given the answers to the questions that she asked; her singing experience was a disaster. She recalls being sent away and treated harshly. However, she was loved.

The parents seem defensive of the treatment that she received and deny the harsh words levelled at them. The parents appear cold and authoritarian: as long as their child was safe they did not seem to care about her emotional needs. Her comic ended up in the fire after an argument. They believe that because they loved her they could do no harm. But the child remembers harsh discipline and a feeling of rejection.

Themes

- Troubled family relationships: children see things differently from their parents.
- Childhood memories: they can affect our whole lives

Structure and Style

- The poem is in six equal stanzas. This consistent, rational shape reflects the rational argument and the rigidity of the parents' point of view.
- The poem has a **conversational tone**, with **short direct sentences**. **Colloquial** phrases are also used
- **Enjambment** represents the argument: it is ongoing, like the lines.
- In stanza four the poem becomes more **authoritarian in tone** and more aggressive.
- **Alliteration**, e.g. 'firm' and 'fear', stresses the treatment the child received, and suggests that the child's impressions are correct.
- The poem has a **circular structure**; it goes round in a circle, like the argument.
- The fifth stanza has an **angry tone** and a **confrontational structure:** a question is asked but is then answered in a confrontational, defensive way
- The **disjointed sentences** suggest that the parents are guilty of the charges their child brings against them – when we try to defend ourselves we speak in a disjointed way.
- The metaphors on lines 16 and 17 highlight how the child feels – that her parents' treatment of her will affect the rest of her life.

Stealing Carol Ann Duffy

Content

The poem's persona shares his thoughts about his life of boredom, telling us what he has stolen in the past. He juxtaposes his thefts with his thoughts about why he steals, and his pointless theft of a snowman.

Feelings, Characters and Relationships

The character has a destructive and negative relationship with society. He has had a difficult life and wants to inflict on others the pain and disappointments that he has had in his life. His extreme boredom is relayed in line 21, where he says he could eat himself out of boredom. He is fed up of the world and feels that nobody understands him.

He is a negative character, but he does reflect on his actions and initially we can feel some sympathy for him. His vulnerability is revealed through simple expressions. But any sympathy we might feel for him dissipates when he reveals that he got a thrill from making children cry (lines 9–10). He has no consideration for other people's feelings, but he is very aware of his own.

Themes

- Disaffected youth.
- Hatred of society and other people: the persona wants to threaten and upset innocent people.
- Boredom: it is the character's boredom that makes him want to steal.
- Violence: the persona begins to turn violent.

Structure and Style

- The title of the poem is written in the **present participle**, highlighting that the behaviour described is ongoing and prevalent in today's society.
- **Short, abrupt sentences** reflect the persona's thought processes.
- The character appears to want to involve the reader. This is shown through the opening line which is presented as a **question** as if in response to an enquiry. At the end of the poem he directly addresses the reader again by posing a **rhetorical question**. It is as if he wants the reader to understand him.
- **Juxtaposition** of **simple**, **colloquial phrases** that reflect real speech, with beautiful images, e.g. 'weighed a ton', 'looked magnificent'.
- **Juxtaposition** of his actions (joy-riding) with his inaction ('to nowhere').
- **Imagery** and **descriptions** suggest the character is not what he appears to be – there is another side to him that can create these wonderful images.
- **Cold diction** is used throughout, e.g. 'frozen', 'chill', which reflects the cruelty of his actions and how he feels inside – cold and numb.
- The **verb** 'hugged' suggests that he was trying to get some comfort from the snowman.
- The poem contains **destructive images**, e.g. in lines 13 and 18 – the persona's anger and frustration are being released.
- The poem begins and ends with an **interrogative** – the character is questioning his actions and inviting the reader to think about his actions and the cause.

Simon Armitage

Simon Armitage

Simon Armitage was born in Huddersfield, West Yorkshire, in 1963. He studied at Portsmouth and Manchester and had a number of jobs, including working as a probation officer and a DJ, before becoming a writer. As well as writing poetry and plays, he writes for television and radio.

Armitage has taught at the University of Leeds and the University of Iowa's Writers' Workshop and now teaches at Manchester Metropolitan University with Carol Ann Duffy.

Armitage still lives in Yorkshire and many of his poems contain references to the North of England, aspects of the Yorkshire dialect, and play on words. Much of Armitage's poetry contains ambiguities. He wants it to be interpreted on a personal level by the reader.

Helpful Hint

Duffy's and Armitage's poems tend to use simple, everyday words rather than 'poetic' words. It is the way in which these words are used that makes the poems interesting and open to interpretation.

Mother, any distance... Simon Armitage

Content

The poem describes a man moving into his new home. He is leaving the safety and security of the family home to live alone. He finds the prospect both daunting and exciting.

The poem is also about the man's relationship with his mother and the way that he is breaking away from his family ties, emotionally and physically.

Feelings, Characters and Relationships

The poem opens with an address to the man's mother. The man recognises that he needs to break free from the mother–son bond. He has a positive relationship with his mother, although it is a slightly suffocating one. She helps her son in the traditional ways associated with a mother – she helps him move house, measuring up for curtains and carpets, but maybe she is too loving and protective of him, as the move to break away from her seems to be a daunting one. His mother seems to have control over him as she is the 'base' to which he reports back.

The man space-walks through the empty bedrooms, which suggests that he is happy in his new home. He reaches for the 'endless sky'. This positive image suggests he welcomes his freedom. But the line is followed by the realisation that he will either, 'fall or fly': either he will succeed in becoming independent or he will fail. However, he has to take the chance.

Themes

- Family relationships and troubled relationships: the strong bond between mother and child, and the difficulties in trying to grow up and break free.
- Growing up: the excitement of moving on and breaking away, physically and emotionally, from your family.
- Love: the intense love between mother and child.

Structure and Style

- The use of the **formal** word 'Mother' shows that the man has respect and admiration for his mother.
- The use of the **present tense** (e.g. 'climb the ladder', 'still pinch') suggests that this breaking away is an ongoing process. It can last a lifetime.

- The poem contains an **extended metaphor** of the tape measure as the umbilical cord that attaches a baby to its mother. This **symbolises** the strong link between the man and his mother.
- **Enjambment** of the lines represents the man's free-flowing thought processes and the ongoing nature of the relationships between parents and their children.
- **Juxtaposition** of images of freedom and restraint: the anchor, and the 'hatch that opens on an endless sky'.
- **Alliteration** of 'fall or fly' stresses the whole point of the poem. When children move away from their parents they can become successfully independent or they can flounder without the safety net of their family.
- His mother has been his anchor and his kite – an anchor has **connotations** of keeping a ship safe but it also keeps it firmly fastened to one place. A kite is something free and without restraints – maybe this is how the man longs to be.
- The use of the words 'acres' and 'prairies' as measuring the distance he would need to be free suggests that they have been very close indeed.

My father thought... Simon Armitage

Content

Armitage recounts the time when he had his ear pierced as a young man. His father mocked him and this upset him. However, when he reached the age of 29, he came to the same decision as his father – he should take the earring out. The poem suggests that, at some point, we all grow up and become a lot like our parents.

Feelings, Characters and Relationships

The poet as a young man has had his ear pierced and his father mocks him. His father says that he is easily led and should have had his nose pierced like a bull instead so that others could lead him about with it. The father is a traditional man with traditional values and attitudes. This is clear through his use of 'bloody queer', which is a double entendre (i.e. it has two meanings) – 'queer' as in strange and also 'queer' as in gay.

The piercing becomes sore: it 'became a wound, and wept'. This refers to how the poet felt after hearing his father's reaction, as much as to the wound itself.

When he is older he metaphorically turns into his father, agreeing that he should take the earring out and leave it out. This shows that we change as we get older and our values change, often coming to resemble those of our parents. The things that we rebelled against become our values too.

The poet is upset when he realises that he has lost his youth, as his own voice echoes that of his father all

those years ago: 'my own voice breaking like a tear'. He sadly accepts that he has grown up.

Themes

- Family relationships.
- Youth and adulthood: the actions of youth and our parents' reactions to them.
- Growing up: getting older and changing our value system (what we believe).
- Memories: the poet remembers the incident vividly.

Structure and Style

- **Colloquial, informal language**, e.g. 'rolled home', **contrasts** with **poetic language**, e.g. 'my own voice breaking like a tear'. The mixture represents his attitude then and his attitude now.
- **Alliteration**, e.g. 'nerve to numb' and 'wound, and wept', stresses words that the poet wants to emphasise.
- The second stanza has a **narrative quality**. Even though it is short, it recounts the story of the ear being pierced to involve the reader in the story.
- **Emotions** are evident throughout the poem. His father's anger opens the poem, and the poet's sadness ends the poem.
- The consistent **rhyme pattern** of the last three lines rhyming in the first two stanzas helps the story to flow and adds to the **lighthearted tone** in these stanzas. The rhyme pattern changes in the third stanza, perhaps to reflect the more **serious tone**.

Homecoming Simon Armitage

Content

The title of this poem is loaded with meaning. Traditionally, a homecoming is a happy, welcoming affair – an event to be celebrated. However, here, the boy (we presume, although it is not stated) is told off by his mother when he returns home as his jacket has been spoilt at school. He is so upset by her reaction that he slips out at midnight (perhaps with the intention of running away) and waits by the phone box for a call, but it does not ring because 'it's sixteen years or so before we'll meet'. This is an ambiguous line that could be interpreted in different ways – a person he meets in the future, or his older self who would perhaps understand his mother's reaction.

His father is waiting by the gate and he 'wants to set things straight'. Is it this minor event that he wants to sort out or a wider issue?

Feelings, Characters and Relationships

The boy is upset by his mother's reaction. He sees her as a 'model of a mother' who does everything right. The opening stanza describes an exercise in learning to trust, and suggests that his mother is the person whom he trusts completely. Yet she lets him down by blaming him for ruining the jacket.

His father is referred to as the 'father figure' which is a stereotypical description. He is the peacemaker who wants to put everything right.

The boy is upset and disappointed in his mother, but later in life he understands (or accepts) her reaction that day.

Themes

- Love and trust.
- Family relationships and troubled relationships: the boy feels let down when his mother blames him.
- Growing up: how we see things differently as we get older and find out who we are.
- Memories: the poet remembers the incident vividly.

Structure and Style

- The poem opens with a **command** (imperative) – 'Think'. Armitage wants the reader to think, hence the **ambiguities** in the poem and the many possible interpretations.
- The **diction** in the second stanza (e.g. 'scuffed and blackened', 'temper') is angry and negative, which **contrasts** with the trust portrayed in the first stanza.
- **Anonymity** (no names), e.g. use of 'those', 'your', 'silhouette', etc., suggests that the poem could represent anyone, not just the speaker's family.
- **Negative diction** is used in the second stanza to describe the trust being broken and the tempers flaring.
- Colours are used to **symbolise** strong emotions, e.g. 'seeing red', 'Blue murder'.
- The final stanza involves the reader again through **conversational language**, e.g. 'there, like this'.
- The spoiled jacket **metaphorically** becomes the boy – he is upset, ruined. At the end of the poem, the jacket still fits. This could mean that he later understands his mother's anger. Or that the relationship with his parents 'still fits' – has it all been sorted out?
- The events are **juxtaposed** through the poem: the jacket getting ruined, and the boy coming to terms with his mother's reaction.

November Simon Armitage

Content

Again, the poem's title is loaded with meaning. November is a cold, desolate month at the end of the year when plants and flowers have died. The speaker and his friend, John, take John's grandmother to a hospital or nursing home. They feel bad about their actions and they rush to park the car to get it over with. They know that she is going there to die and this makes them consider their own mortality and the fact they too will, one day, be in this condition and will die.

Feelings, Characters and Relationships

The poem does not look at the relationship between John and his grandmother, only the relationship of youth and age in general terms.

The narrator and John are obviously close as they share this difficult task and seem to share the same feelings about what they see and do.

The old woman's behaviour is reflective of someone at the end of life – she 'sinks down into her incontinence': she is submissive and has given up.

The narrator and John appear sympathetic to the grandmother's plight but they make cold observations about the vulgarities of old age. They are afraid of what they themselves will become with age. They 'numb' themselves with alcohol because they do not want to face the reality that they too will grow old and die.

Themes

- Death: dealing with the inevitability of death.
- Old age.
- Making the most out of life and trying to find happiness.
- Troubled family relationships: John is finding it difficult to accept his grandmother's old age.

Structure and Style

- The **title** 'November' could represent not only the time of year, but the time in the grandmother's life – she is heading towards the 'winter' of her life.
- **Negative diction** is used throughout the poem to describe old age, e.g. 'pasty bloodless smiles'. This could suggest the poet's own thoughts about old age.
- 'You're shattered' in line 10 refers to the fact that John is 'shattered' both physically and mentally. It shows that the speaker is close to John and recognises his needs.
- The line, 'We can say nothing' reminds the reader that nothing can be done about the ageing process – there is nothing we can say or do to stop it.
- **Positive diction** is used in the final stanza. However, it starts with 'Sometimes', which prevents it from being entirely positive.
- **Imagery** is used throughout: 'we feel the terror of the dusk' – they are scared because darkness symbolises the end of life and the fear of getting old; 'parcel her in the rough blankets' implies they are sending her away and 'wrapping up' her life.
- The line 'It is time John' is **ambiguous:** it could mean simply that it is time to let his grandmother go, or it could mean that time has aged her: time has caused this distressing event.

Exam Preparation

Decide for yourself – at the end of the poem, are the two characters being optimistic (saying that they should make the most out of life) or pessimistic (saying that the one thing that is guaranteed in life is death)?

Kid   Simon Armitage

The poem is a modern day twist on the relationship between Batman and Robin, or any two people where there is an older, more experienced character and a 'kid' who looks up to them and admires everything they do.

The poem deals with the relationship between the 'Batman' and 'Robin' characters. 'Batman' has ordered 'Robin' to grow up and he has done so, realising that 'Batman' is not all he was made out to be. He has faults, like any other person: he had an affair with a married woman and he ages like any other person. He quickly becomes an ex-hero. At the end of the poem we see him portrayed in the younger character's imagination as feeble and struggling.

The poem ends with the 'boy wonder' (the 'kid') being in control. The Batman and Robin analogy represents the relationship between any such characters in life.

Feelings, Characters and Relationships

The relationship between the two characters was one of admiration of the older character by the younger, until the older one told the younger to grow up, and 'ditched' him 'in the gutter'. Originally, the older character acted like an older brother and the younger looked up to him, until he had an affair with a married woman.

The younger character feels disappointment that his 'hero' has turned out to be as normal as anyone else. He feels he has been treated badly by him and delights in seeing him 'stewing over chicken giblets in the pressure cooker'.

Armitage explores how relationships change as we get older and begin to see things differently. 'Batman' has gone from being the 'big shot' in the opening line of the poem to the 'baby' at the end. 'Robin' grows up to be 'taller, harder, stronger' and 'older'.

Themes

- Relationships: how relationships change with time.
- Admiration: the 'hero' is only human after all.
- Youth: we are often deceived in our youth to admire people who are not worthy of our admiration and respect.
- Truth and honesty: the truth about people always comes out in the end.

Structure and style

- The poem's title is again loaded with **connotations:** a kid is childish and innocent.
- The Batman and Robin relationship is **juxtaposed** with the modern day equivalent.
- Typical Batman and Robin phrases are **parodied** (imitated) to highlight the comparison, e.g. in lines 12 and 13.
- **Comic-like phrases** are used, e.g. 'the wild blue yonder', 'Holy robin-redbreast-nest-egg-shocker', with more **colloquial** turns of phrase: 'ditched me, rather, in the gutter'. This **informal style** represents the close relationship between the characters.
- A **jaunty, mocking tone** is achieved through occasional **rhymes,** the 10 syllable lines, and words with a stressed first syllable, e.g. – 'stronger', 'nothing'.
- **Alliteration** emphasises the **sarcastic tone,** e.g.'Batman, big shot', 'ball boy'.
- In lines 15–17, 'Robin' swaps his 'Robin clothes' for normal clothes (jeans and a jumper). This suggests that he has grown up and become his own person. He has swapped fantasy for reality.
- **Imagery** is used throughout, e.g. 'without a shadow' and 'punching the palm of your hand' to stress 'Batman's' new-found loneliness.

Those bastards... Simon Armitage

Content

The poem recounts the persona's anger at rich people and the upper classes. He sees himself as a Robin Hood figure that must right the wrongs of the oppressed classes.

The persona can be seen to represent sections of the youth of today who are becoming an underclass: he has no money, no job and no opportunities.

The poem has a political message – the class divide cannot be accepted and should be challenged or it could result in the eruption of violence.

Feelings, Characters and Relationships

The poem explores the relationships of the social classes. The persona is full of bitter hatred for the landed gentry. His loathing is evident in the opening line and in the negative diction that runs throughout the poem. He is a violent character who feels that he is looked down on. Images of slavery suggest that he feels he is treated as a slave by the upper classes.

However, he compares himself to Prometheus from the Greek legend, a character who stole fire from the gods and gave light to mortals. This suggests that he sees himself as a potential hero of the working classes.

The threat he poses is evident in the last line of the poem, 'Me, I stick to the shadows, carry a gun'. This reminds us of the violent characters in Duffy's poems.

Themes

- Social injustice and inequality: the class divide.
- Hatred of society and other people: the persona has intense hatred for the rich.
- Violence and death: the mention of the gun implies violence and, potentially, death.

Structure and Style

- The poet displays direct anger through the persona: 'Those bastards in their mansions'.
- The poet uses the **third person** to refer to the rich. His use of the **second person** throughout the poem suggests that he is trying to involve the reader and is trying to get the reader on his side.
- **Classical imagery** is used to remind the reader of the Greek myth of Prometheus, to whom the persona compares himself.
- **Imagery** and **diction from the slave trade** is evident in the second stanza, e.g. 'cuffs and shackles', 'iron from their wrists and ankles'. This implies that the persona feels he is regarded as a slave by the rich.
- The poem contains a lot of **aggressive, war diction**, e.g. 'forced', 'burning', 'armed' and 'gun'.
- There are a number of **stereotypes** in the poem, e.g. 'threadbare britches' is a stereotype of the poor; 'beagles' (hounds used for hunting) reinforces the stereotype that rich people go hunting.
- The final line is isolated and direct. This represents the persona in the poem and the feelings he expresses.
- A **tone** of anger and aggression runs throughout the poem, culminating (ending) in the sinister threat of the last line.
- Occasional **rhyme** adds to the build up to the sinister last line.

I've made out a will... Simon Armitage

Content

The theme of death is explored from the first person perspective. The poem catalogues how the speaker is happy to leave all his bodily parts to research, apart from the heart, because the heart symbolises much more than just the organ we find in the body. The heart is the reason for living: the thing that makes us human.

Feelings, Characters and Relationships

The speaker deals with death in a mildly humorous yet matter-of-fact way. He describes his body parts using interesting images. However, the importance of the heart is stressed. The heart is where love, emotions and relationships are kept.

The speaker shows no fear of death: it is treated in a humorous way. However, the last line is ambiguous – it sounds ominous –the heart 'hangs'. Why would the heart be hanging anywhere unless the body that contained it was also hanging?

Themes

- Love and passion: the importance of the heart and emotions in our lives.
- Life and death.
- Finding happiness in life.

Structure and Style

- The poem has an unusual opening line which sets the **tone** for the rest of the poem.
- The use of the **present tense** throughout the poem, and the use of the **present participle** in 'I'm leaving myself', implies that making out the will is an ongoing decision.
- There are a few **images** that refer to food: 'jellies', 'syrups', 'loaf of brains', 'assortment of fillings', 'bilberry soup'. This implies that the body is no more than a set of ingredients.
- An **extended metaphor** of the body as a machine or clock runs throughout the poem, e.g. 'sprockets and springs and rods', 'the cogs and the hands', 'the pendulum'. This highlights the speaker's feeling that the body is unimportant, just parts, and only the heart (which contains emotions and love) is important.
- The **tone** is comic and lighthearted due to the images that are applied to the parts of the body.
- There is a strong **contrast** between the humour of the first stanza, and the seriousness of the final line in the first stanza: 'but not the heart, they can leave that alone'. There is also a vivid **contrast** between the seriousness of the poem's final line, and the general **tone** of the rest of the poem.

Hitcher Simon Armitage

Content

This is a chilling poem about the murder of an innocent hitchhiker from the viewpoint of the murderer.

It is a confessional monologue where the persona tells us about the day of the murder, the murder itself and his actions afterwards. It is narrated with callous detachment (i.e. the persona is not emotionally involved with his actions).

Feelings, Characters and Relationships

The persona is detached from society; he has not been going to work and has been threatened with the sack. He describes himself as 'tired, under the weather'. It appears that he may have carefully planned the murder as he hired a car but, on the other hand, his actions seem unpredictable and erratic.

He recounts the murder with detachment; he has not emotionally engaged with the hitcher. He even callously remarks that the man could walk away from the point that he rolled him out of the car. His humour is chilling and shows how strangely he is acting.

The man is violent, unpredictable and perhaps a manic depressive. Perhaps he feels trapped by his life and envies the hitcher's freedom and lack of responsibility. He shows no remorse when he has killed him.

The hitcher is portrayed as a 'hippy' character, a free spirit who follows the wind and sleeps where he finds himself. He refers to a Bob Dylan song 'blowin' in the wind' and tells the persona that 'he liked the breeze to run its fingers through his hair'. This is a poetic phrase which contrasts with the colloquial, violent language that the persona uses.

Themes

- Violence and death: the murder is pointless.
- Troubled relationships: the persona has a negative relationship with society and with other people.
- Hatred of society and other people.

Structure and Style

- **Personification** of the man's answerphone: it 'kept screaming'. This highlights the man's stress and frustration which, perhaps, lead him to do what he does.
- Specific references and details are given, e.g. 'Vauxhall Astra', 'Leeds', 'top road out of Harrogate', which suggests the man is concerned or obsessed with such details.
- References are made to freedom and the alternative lifestyle of the hitcher. This **contrasts** with the modern technology (the 'ansaphone') that causes the man's stress.
- **Colloquial language** is used by the persona, e.g. 'I let him have it', 'Stitch that'. It is as if he is telling the story to friends, proud of what he has done. The line 'and didn't even swerve' also suggests he feels that what he has done is impressive.
- **Images of violence / violent diction**, e.g. 'once with the head' (a head butt) and 'six times with the krooklok' (steering-wheel lock).
- There is a vivid **contrast** between the language of the murderer and the hitcher, which also shows the contrast of their characters.
- The poem has a mixture of **short and long lines** which represent the man's uneven thought processes and his reflections.
- Some lines have full stops at the end; some run on (**enjambment**). This makes it sound like a real person telling a story.

Comparing Post-1914 Poetry

In the exam you will be asked to compare the poems by Carol Ann Duffy and Simon Armitage both to each other, and to poems from the pre-1914 poetry bank.

The following list shows some of the themes which are common among the poems by Duffy and Armitage. This list will provide a quick reference when you are looking at themes that a number of the poems share.

- **Failed / troubled relationships** – *Havisham, Salome, We Remember Your Childhood Well, Mother, any distance, My father thought, Homecoming, November, Kid* and *Hitcher*.
- **Love and passion** – *Havisham, Anne Hathaway, Before You Were Mine, Mother, any distance* and *I've made out a will*.
- **Memories** – *Havisham, Anne Hathaway, Before You Were Mine, We Remember Your Childhood Well, My father thought* and *Homecoming*.
- **Hatred of society / other people** – *Stealing, Those bastards* and *Hitcher*.
- **Family relationships** – *Elvis's Twin Sister, Before You Were Mine, We Remember Your Childhood Well, Mother, any distance, My father thought, Homecoming* and *November*.
- **Violence / death** – *Havisham, Salome, Stealing, Those bastards, I've made out a will* and *Hitcher*.
- **Finding happiness** – *Elvis's Twin Sister, Anne Hathaway, Before You Were Mine, November* and *I've made out a will*.

The following list shows some structure and style techniques which are common among some of the poems by Duffy and Armitage.

- **Use of well-known characters from history / literature** – *Havisham, Elvis's Twin Sister, Salome, Anne Hathaway* and *Kid*.
- **Use of enjambment** – *Anne Hathaway, Salome, We Remember Your Childhood Well, Mother, any distance* and *Hitcher*.
- **Colloquial language** – *Elvis's Twin Sister, Salome, Before You Were Mine, We Remember Your Childhood Well, Stealing, My father thought, Kid* and *Hitcher*.
- **Use of the present tense** – *Before You Were Mine, Mother, any distance* and *I've made out a will*.
- **Poems which appeal to the senses** – *Havisham, Anne Hathaway* and *Before You Were Mine*.

See pages 74–75 for comparing the poems

by Duffy and Armitage with poems from the pre-1914 poetry bank.

Exam Preparation

Make a list of the common links that you can find among the poems by Duffy and Armitage.

Comparing Pre-1914 and Post-1914 Poetry

In Section B of the exam you will have one hour to answer one question that will ask you to compare the poems that you have read. This means you need to have a clear idea of what the poems have in common. You will have to compare poetry from the pre-1914 poetry bank with post-1914 poetry by Carol Ann Duffy and Simon Armitage. You could be asked to compare any of the following:

- **Content:** what is happening in the poems.
- **Setting:** where and when the events in the poems take place.
- **Themes:** what the poems are about.
- **Structure and form:** are the poems sonnets, free verse, etc.? How are they arranged? Think about stanzas, line length, and the shape of the poems. How does the structure relate to each poem's content?
- **Language and style,** for example…
  - voice: who is speaking? Are the poems written in the first, second or third person? Why?
  - rhythm and metre: what rhythm is there and how does it help to convey meaning?
  - rhyme: what rhyme patterns are there? How does the rhyme affect the tone of the poems?
  - diction: is it modern or archaic? Is it unusual in any way?
  - imagery: the pictures the poets create through words. Look at metaphors and similes. Do the poets' images have anything in common?
  - techniques: how do devices such as alliteration and onomatopoeia contribute to the effect that the poem has on the reader?

The following example question will give you an idea of what you may be asked to do.

Q. (a) Compare how feelings towards loved ones are shown in any two of these poems:
> *Before You Were Mine* (Duffy)
> *Mother, any distance* (Armitage)
> *Homecoming* (Armitage)

and then

(b) Compare how feelings towards loved ones are shown in any two of these poems:
> *On My First Sonne* (Jonson)
> *The Affliction of Margaret* (Wordsworth)
> *Sonnet 130* (Shakespeare)

In both parts (a) and (b), remember to compare…
- the feelings towards loved ones in the poems
- how the poets show these feelings.

You need to be aware of the similarities and differences between the poems in order to answer the questions. The question above asks you for…
- descriptions of the feelings towards loved ones in the four poems that you have chosen from the options given
- explanations and evidence of how the writers use structure and language (and perhaps context and setting) to convey these feelings
- similarities and differences between the feelings towards loved ones that are shown in the poems
- similarities and differences between how the writers use structure and language (and perhaps context and setting) to convey these feelings.

To answer this question successfully, you need to choose two poems from each list that you know well and can write a lot about.

Your answers to part (a) and part (b) should each include a short introduction which is relevant to the question. You should write in the introductions which two poems you will be comparing. You should then go on to compare the poems.

You could conclude your answers by giving your overall opinion, e.g. whether the feelings are similar or different, or whether the language techniques used in one poem convey the feelings more effectively than the other.

Table 1 below lists three different themes. It also names the poems from the pre-1914 poetry bank and the poems by Carol Ann Duffy and Simon Armitage which are linked by each theme.

Table 2 suggests some poems by Duffy and Armitage that could be effectively linked to each poem from the pre-1914 poetry bank.

Exam Practice

Choose one of the themes in Table 1. Then choose two poems from the pre-1914 poetry list, and two poems from the Duffy and Armitage list, and write about how the theme is portrayed in each of the four poems through the way the poets write.

Exam Preparation

Consider how the poems in Table 2 are linked and try to write about their similarities and differences.

Table 1

Theme	Pre-1914 Poems	Post-1914 Poems: Duffy and Armitage
Love / Passion	On My First Sonne, The Affliction of Margaret, Sonnet 130, My Last Duchess, The Laboratory, Sonnet	Havisham, Anne Hathaway, Before You Were Mine, Mother, any distance, I've made out a will
Violence / Death	On My First Sonne, The Affliction of Margaret, Tichborne's Elegy, The Man He Killed, My Last Duchess, The Laboratory, Ulysses	Havisham, Salome, Stealing, Those bastards, I've made out a will, Hitcher
Family Relationships	On My First Sonne, The Affliction of Margaret, The Little Boy Lost and The Little Boy Found, Ulysses	Elvis's Twin Sister, Before You Were Mine, We Remember Your Childhood Well, Mother, any distance, My father thought, Homecoming, November

Table 2

Pre-1914 Poems	Post-1914 Poems: Duffy and Armitage
On My First Sonne	Anne Hathaway, Before You Were Mine, My father thought
The Song of the Old Mother	Anne Hathaway, Mother, any distance, November
The Affliction of Margaret	Havisham, Mother, any distance, Homecoming
The Little Boy Lost and The Little Boy Found	Before You Were Mine, We Remember Your Childhood Well, My father thought, Homecoming
Tichborne's Elegy	Anne Hathaway, November, I've made out a will
The Man He Killed	Salome, Stealing, Hitcher
Patrolling Barnegat	November
Sonnet 130	Anne Hathaway, Before You Were Mine
My Last Duchess	Havisham, Elvis's Twin Sister, Salome, Those bastards, Hitcher
The Laboratory	Salome, Stealing, Those bastards, Hitcher
Ulysses	Havisham, Anne Hathaway, Salome, November, Kid
The Village Schoolmaster	We Remember Your Childhood Well, Homecoming
The Eagle	Those bastards
Inversnaid	Mother, any distance, November, Kid
Sonnet	Anne Hathaway

Exam Tips

When writing your answer, you could write about one poem, then the other, and then make a comparison in your final paragraph. However, it is far better to compare the poems simultaneously as you work through your answer, dealing with a different aspect of both poems (content, themes, structure, language), one at a time. Remember that you are looking for similarities and differences between the poems.

You must use the **PEE** technique (**P**oint, **E**vidence, **E**xplanation), choosing brief but relevant quotations from the text.

Before the exam, make sure that you...
- know each poem well. Read each poem at least five times and make sure you understand what is happening in each one
- know the meaning of any unfamiliar words
- have annotated the poems well
- have come up with your own ideas about the poems – the examiner wants to see your personal opinions
- have completed all the 'Exam Preparation' and 'Exam Practice' tasks given in this section of the guide

- have completed at least three past exam questions
- have perfected the PEE technique (see page 11)
- are able to write confidently about content, settings, themes, structure and style.

In the exam, make sure that you...
- are aware of the time: you only have **one hour** to complete Section B. It is helpful to spend about five minutes planning what you are going to write
- read the questions carefully: choose one that you fully understand and that you can answer well
- annotate (highlight) the poems that you will use in your answer, keeping the question at the front of your mind
- use the bullet points in the question to help you write your answer.

Helpful Hint

Try to write about poems that you enjoy and understand fully. You will probably have more to say about them and your enthusiasm will show in your answer.

Exam Practice

Answer each of the following exam practice questions in one hour and ask your teacher to grade them. Remember to highlight the key words in the questions and use the PEE technique in your answers.

Q. Compare the ways in which the poets use the first person to tell us about other people's lives in **two** poems from list A and **two** poems from list B:

List A
Elvis's Twin Sister (Duffy)
Salome (Duffy)
Hitcher (Armitage)

List B
The Song of the Old Mother (Yeats)
My Last Duchess (Browning)
The Laboratory (Browning)

Q. Answer **both** parts (a) and (b).

(a) Compare how the poets present the relationship between a parent and a child in *Mother, any distance* by Simon Armitage and in **one** poem from the pre-1914 poetry bank.

and then

(b) Compare how parent–child relationships are presented in *Before You Were Mine* by Carol Ann Duffy and one more poem from the pre-1914 poetry bank.

Q. Compare how the poets write about violence in *Salome* by Carol Ann Duffy, **one** poem by Simon Armitage, and **two** poems from the pre-1914 poetry bank.

Helpful Hint

Many of the questions in Section B of the exam have two parts to them: (a) and (b). Make sure that you answer both parts. If you only answer one part, you can only achieve a maximum of half the marks available for Section B of the English Literature exam.

Developing Your Answer

Below is an example answer to the following question.

Q. Compare the ways in which the poets use the first person to tell us about other people's lives in **two** poems from list A and **two** poems from list B:

List A
Havisham (Duffy)
Salome (Duffy)
Kid (Armitage)

List B
The Affliction of Margaret (Wordsworth)
My Last Duchess (Browning)
Ulysses (Tennyson)

Introduces the four poems to be discussed and links their subject matter, focusing on the question

Both 'Salome' and 'Havisham' by Carol Ann Duffy give a personal voice to well-known characters from history or literature: 'Salome' from the Bible and Miss Havisham from Charles Dickens's novel 'Great Expectations'. Tennyson and Browning also use the first person to explore the feelings of characters from history. Tennyson's 'Ulysses' is about the mythical hero of Homer's 'Odyssey', while the persona adopted in 'My Last Duchess' is not as well-known but is still based on a real person (the 16th century Duke of Ferrara).

The most striking aspect of the Duffy poems is that both characters are very hostile towards men. Salome, the stepdaughter of King Herod, demanded the head of John the Baptist as a reward for her dancing whilst Miss Havisham, having been jilted by her fiancé, shut herself away forever still wearing her wedding dress. We need to know something about the stories before reading the poems, as the poet does not 're-tell' them in detail.

Correct language terms are used to make points

Havisham's attitude to men is obvious straightaway by the use of 'Beloved' and 'bastard' in the same sentence. This oxymoron and the violent language shows her love–hate relationship with the man who left her. The first stanza vividly describes her anger and how it has hardened her and made her bitter. She uses 'ropes' as a metaphor to describe the appearance of veins on her old hands, telling us how long she has lived with this hatred. She extends the metaphor to express the violence of her feelings in a quite horrific image of using her veins to kill him. In the second stanza she seems to feel sorry for herself. The single word 'Spinster' emphasises her sense of rejection and failure. The wedding dress is a symbol of her lost youth and happiness. In the third stanza she speaks of her dreams of love, but she comes back to reality in the final stanza, when she expresses her hatred by contrasting happy images of a wedding ('veil', 'cake') with images of violence: 'stabbed'.

Connectives are used to link sentences and paragraphs

PEE is used

Like 'Havisham', 'Salome' has four stanzas, but the poem is not as regular; each stanza has a different number of lines of varying lengths, whereas in 'Havisham' the lines and stanzas are all the same length. This difference reflects a difference between the characters of the speakers. While Havisham is trying to control her feelings and is looking back on the events of a long time ago, Salome seems to be describing very recent events. She is not in control of her thoughts, which seem to develop as she wakes up.

Quotes are used as part of PEE to prove the points that are made

The language of 'Salome', like that of 'Havisham', is quite informal and chatty, although at the beginning it is not nearly as violent or bitter. Salome speaks in a very modern way, using phrases such as 'good-looking', 'on the batter' and 'I'd guess'. She talks about everyday things like having breakfast and, like a modern woman who drinks too much, vows to 'clean up my act'. Whereas Havisham expresses her feelings towards men directly using violent language, Salome's diction is cool and casual. Salome's violent act seems to be part of everyday life for her as she reveals at the end that in her bed is the man's 'head on a platter'. The reader is shocked by Salome's lack of feeling as much as by the horror of the image.

Personal opinions are given

Quotes are used to prove points

This answer is structured into logical paragraphs, and personal opinions are given throughout. Notice how the two post-1914 poems from List A are discussed together and then, how the two pre-1914 poems from List B are introduced and all four poems are discussed together.

Helpful Hint

You need to show that you are aware of the content, context, themes, structure and style of the poems you write about in your answer.

Correct language terms are used to make points

Like Duffy, Tennyson and Browning use the first person to explore the minds of people who have had extraordinary lives. The themes of 'My Last Duchess' have a lot in common with those of 'Salome' and 'Havisham'. 'My Last Duchess' is also about the relationships between men and women, although here, it is from the man's point of view. Like 'Salome', it features a person talking about violent deeds in a down-to-earth, casual way. Also, like Duffy, Browning gradually reveals what the speaker has done. The Duke has killed his wife because of his suspicions ('she lik'd / whate'er she looked on') and jealousy, while Salome has killed her lover because he did not respond to her advances; he was 'colder than pewter' when she kissed him. In both cases their motives are sexual, like Havisham's.

Connectives are used to link sentences and paragraphs

'My Last Duchess' is a dramatic monologue in which the Duke talks to an unheard listener. Like 'Salome', the Duke gives his version of the story, and in doing so, he reveals a lot about himself. Also, like Salome, he seems to have no sense of having done anything wrong. The poem's form is more regular and controlled than 'Salome' – more like 'Havisham'. It is written in iambic pentameters. The regularity of the metre and the rhyme might reflect the Duke's calmness and control, which contrast with his violent acts.

PEE is used

Tennyson's 'Ulysses' is also a dramatic monologue, which explores the mind of a mythical figure in the same way that 'Salome' explores the mind of a biblical figure. However, in this case the subject of the poem is a heroic figure whose character and deeds have been praised and admired by all. Like 'Havisham', the poem is about a person looking back, but here he does not look back with regret. His life is not over. He is restless and wants to go on a final adventure. Like Havisham, he feels trapped in his present life but, unlike her, he is neither bitter about his past nor accepting. He wants to 'drink life to the lees'.

Quotes are used as part of PEE to prove the points that are made

Like 'My Last Duchess', 'Ulysses' is written in iambic pentameters, but this poem does not rhyme, making it flow more, conveying the desire for freedom that 'Ulysses' feels. He uses vivid imagery to describe his past experiences. He speaks of his 'hungry heart' and his 'drunk delight'; he wants to 'shine' rather than 'rust'.

Personal opinions are given

'Ulysses' does not tell a story – in this sense it is like 'Havisham' and 'Salome', assuming that we know the story. Instead, we follow his mood from discontent to enthusiasm and determination 'to strive, to seek, to find and not to yield.' It differs, however, from the other three poems in that Ulysses has a much more positive outlook on life and looks forward to his future, even to his own death: 'To sail beyond the sunset, and the baths / Of all the western stars, until I die.' He will not fear death if he has seen the world.

Quotes are used to prove points

Conclusion links all four poems and refers back to the question

All four poems employ the first person to give a voice to characters from literature or history and to explore their emotions and thoughts on particular events, but Duffy and Browning write about the dark and violent side of human nature, whereas Tennyson's outlook is more positive and life-affirming.

Index